A THEORY OF GENERICIZATION ON BRAND NAME CHANGE

A THEORY OF GENERICIZATION ON BRAND NAME CHANGE

Shawn M. Clankie

Studies in Onomastics
Volume 6

The Edwin Mellen Press
Lewiston•Queenston•Lampeter

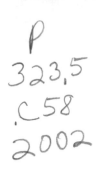

P
323.5
.C58
2002

Library of Congress Cataloging-in-Publication Data

Clankie, Shawn.
   A theory of genericization on brand name change / Shawn M. Clankie.
     p. cm. -- (Studies in onomastics ; v. 6)
   Includes bibliographical references and index.
   ISBN-0-7734-6955-9
    1. Onomastics. 2. Brand name products. 3. Generic products. I. Title. II. Series.

   P323.5 .C58 2002
   929.9'7--dc21

                              2002070180

This is volume 6 in the continuing series
Studies in Onomastics
Volume 6 ISBN 0-7734-6955-9
SO Series ISBN 0-7734-7725-X

A CIP catalog record for this book is available from the British Library.

Copyright © 2002   Shawn M. Clankie

The Edwin Mellen Press
Box 450
Lewiston, New York
USA 14092-0450

The Edwin Mellen Press
Box 67
Queenston, Ontario
CANADA L0S 1L0

The Edwin Mellen Press, Ltd.
Lampeter, Ceredigion, Wales
UNITED KINGDOM SA48 8LT

Printed in the United States of America

To my parents

TABLE OF CONTENTS

LIST OF TABLES

LIST OF FIGURES

PREFACE

In the 1950s one of Arthur Godfrey's television programs was sponsored by *Frigidaire* and during commercials Godfrey would admonish his viewers, "Don't say you're going to buy a new *Frigidaire* and then go out and buy any old refrigerator. Make sure it's a genuine *Frigidaire*." Several decades later Bill Cosby pitched the virtues of *Jello* brand gelatin, and the Coca-Cola company took to court restaurants who served Pepsi to their customers who had asked for a *Coke*. *Frigidaire*, *Jello*, and *Coke* were players in a sociolinguistic game long thought to be of little interest and even less consequence.

Like most linguists and students of the English language, I was brought up to believe that the process whereby brand names, once proper nouns, became generic, common nouns was simple and straightforward, and part of a more general semantic expansion or extension of meaning; *aspirin*, *kleenex*, and *xerox* were common examples. And it was usually brought out that these were often dialect-specific, like *hoover* in British English, which is the general name for the machine and for the act of vacuuming itself, unknown to most Americans except those who have lived in Britain or taken a class in linguistics where it is a preferred example.

All of these examples (and there are hundreds in English) were presented as individual examples of the process of genericization, but there was no known system or pattern underlying it; some brand names, such as *Xerox*, quickly became generic not only as nouns but as verbs and adjectives as well, while others, such as *Sony* and *Ford*, did not. No one thought it would be of any great interest to investigate why *Frigidaire* became the general name for all refrigerators in the second quarter of the 20th century while the names of its competitors such as *Westinghouse* and *Kenmore*, and even *Coldspot*, did not. In other words, some brand names simply became generic, in spite of the time, money, and effort spent by corporations to keep them from doing so while others did not and the reasons behind the changes were trivial and unimportant.

It is with great pleasure that I welcome Shawn Clankie's investigation of genericization, which shows conclusively that there is indeed a system underlying the journey from brand name to generic and offers preliminary answers to such questions as why do some brand names become generic while others do not and what are the limits (if any) on the path, linguistically and socially, that the process must take.

In addition, Clankie does a great service to onomastics since he puts the study of names on a firm scientific footing and provides a framework which can be applied to other onomastic investigations and indeed to the general study of language in society. As a discipline, and especially in the English-speaking world, onomastics has lagged behind its sister disciplines in developing a rigorous theory and methodology. Onomasts have been content to treat names as isolated items and we have done a good job of ferreting out the language origins of the names of people and places and tracing their development over time and space, but we have developed few general principles of naming and we know very little about the linguistic and social constraints on names and naming. Names of all sorts (personal names, geographic names, product names) are in constant competition with one another and Clankie has shown us that there are general principles involved which have a great deal to say about which names will be the winners and which will be the losers; in other words there is indeed a structured process whereby a proper noun (proper adjective, really, to use Clankie's term) breaks loose from its moorings and becomes a class name, then perhaps a verb and an adjective as well. This is the great strength of Clankie's work; not only does he provide novel insights into the process of genericization, he gives to onomastics both a vision (that a small set of principles governs much of naming behavior) and a procedure whereby these principles can be rigorously tested. I know of only 3 or 4 other instances where such an elaborated program for onomastics has been made available. In this sense, Clankie's is a ground-breaking effort with great potential for influencing the form and practice of name study in the future.

In this book Clankie considers a number of important issues: brand names and the law, the relationship of names to other lexical items, cross-cultural aspects of brand names and genericization, and the social foundations of names.

There are many more aspects to the genericization of brand names, of course; there are obvious regional dimensions, along with social, situational, and contextual dimensions. For instance, Thomas E. Murray, in an article in *Names: A Journal of Onomastics* (September 1995) traces the regional and temporal path of *Coke* from brand name to would be generic. Even though the Coca-Cola company prides itself on its efforts to preserve the name *Coke* as a brand name, it has met with limited success and from the referents we can glimpse a brand name change in progress: for some people, *Coke* means exactly what the Cola-Cola company claims it should mean-a cola beverage produced by the Coca-Cola company; for others, however, it means any cola-type drink, and for still others it has become fully generic and means any soft drink, cola or not. Clankie's work should inspire research into these and other aspects of the competition among names.

Clankie's investigation is important to onomastics for several reasons, first among these is a reaffirmation of the notion that language is independent of the legal or artificial social constraints placed upon it. While this can be seen so clearly in the case of brand name genericization, it is perplexing that institutions, in spite of all historical precedent, still strive mightily to 'defend' the language against the people who use it.

Second, and perhaps more far reaching for onomastics, Clankie makes clear that the people, even though they know the language intimately and they are the ultimate creators of the forms it eventually takes, are themselves constrained by abstract principles of the language they use.

Edward Callary

Editor, *Names: A Journal of Onomastics*

Past President, American Name Society

FOREWORD

Genericization is the process by which a brand name, specific in reference, undergoes a series of grammatical and semantic changes to become a common class-noun representative of the entire semantic class to which that product belongs. *Kleenex tissues--> a kleenex, Xerox photocopiers--> a xerox* or *to xerox* demonstrate this process. The theory put forth contains four hypotheses based upon both the characteristics that contribute to the occurrence of genericization and the belief that genericization is a regular process. The first of these hypotheses maintains that genericization will occur in novel semantic classes. The second hypothesis focuses on brand versus class-noun length, arguing that the shorter the brand name in relation to the class-noun, the greater the likelihood for genericization to occur. The third hypothesis insists that genericization is a regular hierarchical process. Finally, the fourth hypothesis states that for a brand name to become generic there must be an association to a single product.

To test the four hypotheses, a corpus of one hundred generic brand names was constructed. Sixty-one of the one hundred generic names in the corpus were selected from previous articles noting the names as generic. Each of these sixty-one names was then cross-checked for a minimum of two generic examples in the Oxford English Dictionary (2nd Ed.) and through generic use as found on the Internet. To complete the corpus, an additional thirty-nine names not found in previous work were added on the basis of the same criteria. Each of the one hundred names was then run against individualized tests in an attempt to disprove the four hypotheses. The results of the tests were then charted and analyzed. It was discovered that Hypotheses 1, 2, and 4 were shown to be supported by the data, and Hypothesis 3 (the process of genericization) required a single vi

modification to reflect more accurately the process that takes place when genericization occurs.

   Once the analysis was undertaken for this corpus built from English examples, consideration was then given (1) to genericization cross-linguistically with Japanese as the example, and (2) to the problems of proprietary status. Finally, a practical application of the results was created to assist companies in producing brand names that are less likely to undergo genericization.

PART I: FOUNDATIONS

CHAPTER I. INTRODUCTION

The difference between the almost-right word & the right word is really a large matter-- it's the difference between the lightning bug and the lightning.
-Mark Twain (Letter to George Bainton, October 15, 1888).

1.1 The Problem

1.1.1 Background

The brand name, as a reflection of the material nature of Western capitalist culture, is among the most pervasive descriptive elements in American English. Throughout our daily lives we are confronted with brand upon brand. We wake up to our breakfast of a cup of *Folger's* coffee served with *Meadow Gold* milk and *NutraSweet* sweetener, our *Aunt Jemima* pancakes topped with Smucker's jam and a dab of *Land-o-Lakes* butter, all accompanied by two strips of *Oscar Mayer* bacon. While eating, we turn on our television and are told to have a *Bud Light*, drive a *Chevy*, and to send our packages by *Federal Express* (now FedEx). A look at the newspaper shows that *Coca-Cola* and *Spam* are on sale at *Long's* Drug, and that there are sales at *J. C. Penney's*, *Chanel*, and *Liberty House*. Even the forks and spoons used to eat breakfast are brought to us by *Oneida*. As a matter of fact, everything on the table is branded by the company that produced it.

Before our day has even begun we are faced with a very large number of brand names. Given a 15-hour day, then exposure to brand names multiplies greatly. Calculating an exposure to an average of, say, 300 brand names an hour (a purely arbitrary and perhaps conservative estimate given the available media for advertising), in a 15-hour day the exposure total for a single day would be 4500 tokens. In turn multiplying that number by 365 days, we would find a yearly exposure to 1,642,500 tokens. Of course, many of these are repetitive and others ignored, but the fact remains that we are bombarded with brand names.

Brand-conscious consumers go for the current buzzwords: *Cartier, Ferragamo, Banana Republic,* and so on. At the same time, being inundated with brand names results in a brand-numb public. We are confronted with brand names to the extent that we no longer realize all of the brand names as such. With such proliferation comes inevitable infiltration into the spoken and written language as the brands begin to change in both form and meaning. Some brand names are used so frequently that they become new lexemes, those with an extended semantic range, covering not simply the product produced by a given company, but rather the entire semantic class that the product participates in. It is from this realization that the inspiration for this research program developed.

The epigraph of this chapter exemplifies the intent of my original study (Clankie, 1999), which first drew my interest to the study of brand names. The search for the 'right word' in my own creative writing endeavors led me to attempt to reflect the dialogue and description of my characters as reflective of the spoken language, and to emulate that speech in my own writing. While the genre of writing I'm referring to here, that of short stories and essays, differs significantly from the academic writing we are responsible for as linguists, the search for the right word remains nonetheless important. If presented with a sentence such as *The day-glo laces on the shoes of the little girls seemed to dance like butterflies as they ran across the playground,* where *day-glo* has a significant descriptive value, we can see that the value *day-glo* gives is an emotive value that similar lexemes (fluorescent, incandescent, etc.) do not share. Etymologically, the adjective *day-*

glo comes from the brand name (a proper adjective) *Day-Glo*. Yet, it was uses such as that of the above example which turned out to be quite controversial and to some a violation of trademark law (see for example the Lanham Act of 1946, Trademark Revision Act of 1988, and the Federal Trademark Dilution Act of 1995). On linguistic grounds I have argued that such uses no longer reflect the brand name, but rather separate lexical items (common nouns, verbs, and common adjectives), outside the scope of proprietary law (Clankie 1999). While the subject remains under considerable debate as part of a much larger issue of intellectual property in a number of domains within and outside of academe (lexicography, technology, and of course business), little work has been done on brand names and more precisely, on the types, causes, and motivations of generic change in brand names. Much that has been written on brand names has been done by those in business, by legal counsels, and by those trying to protect their own brand name. These articles are often highly subjective and selective in their coverage, offering little more than prescriptive warning of what should or should not be done with a brand name. Linguists who have written on brand names have frequently focused on single cases such as the widening scope of proprietary law (Lentine and Shuy 1990), or have only mentioned brand name usage in passing (Bolinger 1980) or in short essays within onomastics (Nuessel 1992; Kaplan and Bernays 1997). Perhaps the most significant work done on the subject has been the series of papers and subsequent book of Friedman 1985, 1986a, 1986b, and 1991, who has, through studies of hit plays, newspapers, and novels, shown significant increases in brand name usage in American and British English over the past thirty years.

Lexicographers too have had to deal with an inherent problem associated with brand names, the problem of representing functionally the language as it is used, versus the legal push of companies (many of which now own the publishing houses) to protect their brand. While most dictionaries contain a disclaimer stating that they are making no judgment about the proprietary status of brand

6

names represented as separate lexemes, some lexicographers have taken a decidedly negative view of this practice (see particularly Landau 1994: 395).

That little has been done linguistically on brand names may lead some to believe that it is an unworthy or unsuitable topic for linguistic inquiry. I believe this is a false assumption. Rather, I would like to suggest that the subject has been overlooked by linguists trained in either formalism or functionalism. Perhaps, brand names have simply been considered proper nouns (rather than proper adjectives), or perhaps it has taken someone who has grown up with cable television (a Generation X-er) to realize the full impact that brand names have had upon language.

The relevance of a detailed study on brand names and of a theory of generic brand-name change will have significant implications for not only linguists in terms of language change and language policy, but also for lexicographers and the business and legal communities. As a result of the increasing presence of other proprietary domains in language in other arenas, namely the domain of Internet addresses, which are being treated in a manner similar to that of brand names (Sanders 1996, Clankie 2001), this study will be particularly relevant to anyone interested in the creation, use, and regulation of the name.

Ultimately, this book will be of interest to anyone interested in naming and the way that we use language to reflect one type of naming, that of the brand name.

1.1.2 What are Brand Names?

What is a <u>brand name</u> or <u>brand</u>[1]? Intuitively, <u>brand names</u> are synonymous with <u>product names</u>, yet many <u>company names</u> are also brand names,

---

[1] The difference between the 'brand name' and the 'brand', as I will be using it here, is one of formality. The latter is more colloquial (here an elliptical form from *brand name* not to be confused with the *brand* of a ranch or other senses of the term (as will be discussed in Section 2.1 to follow)), yet both are acknowledged in scholarly work and are interchangeable, just as with

as are names given to <u>services</u>. It is important to distinguish what I am including as a brand name and what I am not. Brand names are a particular type of trademark and the terms <u>brand name</u> and <u>trademark</u> are used synonymously (and will be used interchangeably for the purposes of this book). The trademark however, carries a broader scope of reference which includes not only brand names, but also registered logos (e.g., the Nike swoosh), slogans (e.g., Yo quiero Taco Bell), and package designs (e.g., the bottle design of the Perrier bottle). Brand names however, are more narrow in scope. These names can be divided into three categories; <u>dual-function trade names</u>, which serve both as a company name and brand name, <u>standard brand names</u>, which differ from the company name, and <u>service marks</u>. To explore this further, <u>trade names</u> are company names (e.g., Kimberly-Clark, General Mills, etc.). However, some trade names are also brand names (dual function trade names). *Coca-Cola* for example, is a product of The Coca-Cola Company.

The standard type of brand name is one that is different from the company name (*Kleenex* and *Cheerios* for Kimberly-Clark and General Mills respectively).

A third type of brand name is the <u>service mark</u>. The difference here is that this type of brand name represents a particular company's service as opposed to its tangible product (e.g., *American Express Financial Services*). As with the frequent overlap between trade names and trademarks (brand names), the same overlap arises with trade names and service marks). The example above, *American Express Financial Services*, is the brand name of American Express.

In this body of work, I will be considering brand names of all three of the categories delineated thus far. As some trade names are also brand names, I will consider those trade names which meet that specific qualification. In particular, trade names that are not also brand names will not be included. Both types of brand names, and service marks, will be examined in this study. The other types

---

'brand name' and 'trademark'. They will be used interchangeably throughout the work, and only to refer to registered brand names.

of trademarks noted at the onset of this section (i.e., logos, slogans, etc.) will however be excluded.

1.1.3 Why Study Brand Names?

The question which now arises is, why study brand names? What makes brand names unique? To begin, brand names in English have a number of unique properties which make them a valid subject of inquiry, and each will be examined separately.

First, brand names--that is, all brand names in American and British English--have a visible actuation date which can be tracked. As long as one knows the company that has produced the brand, it is possible to date the introduction of the brand name. This is interesting in that it is one of the few areas in language where we know with great certainty how long a form has been in existence. In ascertaining this information, there are a number of ways of finding the date of creation. These include the *Oxford English Dictionary*, a number of on-line and full-text databases (the Trademarkscan database, Nexis, the Thomas Register, ABI/Inform Power Pages, etc.), the International Trademark Association, manufacturer's directories such as the American Manufacturers Directory, or direct contact with the company. While the date of creation alone is little more than trivial, this information can be useful when it comes to extended senses of meaning and innovative uses. In general, it is extremely difficult to determine when most lexical items entered the language. The OED is likely the best source for etymological data, yet much of this data is based upon the earliest identifiable form in the written language. Thus, it is surely likely that other forms did exist prior to the earliest identified form. While this is a minor problem, we can be much more certain of the date brand names were introduced to the public. The implications of this point will be examined in greater depth in the analysis section.

Directly related to the previous point is that because brand names are created with a specific purpose (that of naming a given product or service), and are governed by guidelines of the law and by groups like the International Trademark Association (INTA), all brand names in English follow, at least initially, a prescribed grammatical pattern. The pattern all brand names are prescribed to follow consists of a proper adjective followed by a common (generic) class-noun, as in *Xerox* copiers, or *Jell-O* gelatin. As all brand names in English follow this pattern, tracking the change in brand names is relatively straightforward. Yet, while the nature of brand names provides us with a convenient, equal starting point for all brand names, not all brand names change, and, of those that do, one must wonder whether all change in the same ways.

A further point worth noting once again is that the proliferation of brand names in the language allows easy identification and an ample supply of data. Moreover, corpora of brand names are available. The INTA Trademark Checklist 1994, which will be employed here, contains 4,000 of the more common ones, each with its generic class-noun.

Finally, the study of brand names goes beyond simply the domain of linguistic research, and will be of interest to both linguists and nonlinguists alike.

1.1.4 Goals of this Volume

First, to fully understand brand names we will need to examine the process of forming brand names. This will be explained in greater detail below. Then, as a consequence of the lack of extensive studies on both lexical change and brand names, some understanding of the types of changes a brand name can undergo in English will need to be established. This examination of brand-name change will consist of the examination of a given corpus of data. Once an understanding of the major grammatical and semantic changes involving brand names in English is established, then in Chapters 5 and 6 I will turn the discussion towards a theory of genericization (semantic broadening in brand names from specific to generic). The theory will be applied to try to account for why some brand names become generic and others do not, what the contributing factors are (both linguistic and nonlinguistic) to genericization, and how companies, through the way they are creating the names, are ultimately responsible for generic brand-name change. Once the theory has been put forward I will examine brand names across languages (both borrowed brand names and native names) to determine whether we can establish any cross-linguistic generalizations. For this chapter (Chapter 7), data from Japanese will be examined. This will be followed an examination of the legal questions and problems raised by proprietary law, and the conclusions. While the goals to this point are only outlined here, in a later section of this chapter I will discuss each of the proposed chapters individually.

1.2 The Approach

1.2.1 Principles of Change

While the very nature of this book as a practical application is not bound by a single theoretical framework beyond that which I will be proposing, it draws upon principles generally accepted in linguistics as well as ideas from cultural studies and translation (Yanabu 1996). The fact that this volume does not adhere to an established theoretical framework is not unusual in sociolinguistics. Charles Ferguson, for one, is widely recognized within sociolinguistics as a defender of such an approach. Writing as the primary author in Enkvist et al. (1992: 46) Ferguson notes the following:

> Sociolinguistics has never been a unified field, and most researchers do not try to construct--or even imagine--a single comprehensive theory of language-in-society. This is partly because the phenomena can be approached from many perspectives and the principal goals of different theoreticians would be quite different. One way to characterize different

approaches is roughly in terms of the size of the phenomena to be investigated, and the terms "macro-sociolinguistics" and "micro-sociolinguistics" are sometimes used in this way (Enkvist et al. in Ferguson 1996:6).

The differentiation made by Ferguson in the quote above, that of macro-sociolinguistics versus micro-sociolinguistics, is an important one to understanding where I place myself within the discipline of sociolinguistics. It should come as little surprise to those who read my work that my primary concern is the application of linguistic theory to larger issues both within and outside of linguistics, whether through language use, language planning, or language rights. My work is therefore decidedly macro-linguistic in nature. This present study is a reflection of that position.

In language change, because there are such a large number of different kinds of change, principles from a number of branches of linguistics will need to be considered. Turning first to semantic change, as it will deal greatly with the theory of genericization I will be advancing, it was Bloomfield 1933 who established a list of nine types of semantic change (narrowing, widening, metaphor, metonymy, synecdoche, hyperbole, litotes, degeneration, and elevation) of which only *widening* (*broadening* will be the term I use throughout) will be important for my work. Similarly, as I am working on word-level distinctions (as opposed to sentential or discourse-centered studies), studies in lexical change will be important. To this end, studies on the search for lexical universals such as Brown and Witkowski 1981 and approaches to universal semantic primitives such as Goddard and Wierzbicka 1994 will be of value. Other more general treatises of language change will serve as valuable reference sources as well. These include McMahon's 1994 discussions on lexical and semantic change, and Grace's 1993 hypothesis of language change as a result of changes in one's knowledge of language (KOL). Additional studies will be covered in each of the chapter briefs following.

In the descriptivist tradition of grammatical analysis in linguistics, principles and categories of grammatical description, namely traditional grammatical categories (noun, verb, adjective, etc.), will be employed throughout.

1.2.2 Data Collection and Examination

As noted earlier in this chapter, there is no shortage of brand names to examine. Actually, rather than having a problem of types and tokens to examine, one must limit in some way the types of brand names to be included in the study. The INTA corpus, consisting of roughly 4000 brand names, will be a convenient starting point. From these, some general exclusions in the selection of brand name classes can be made. First, I propose to exclude brand names and brand name classes not normally in the public domain. These include for example the semantic class of pharmaceuticals and chemical names not accessible outside the medical profession. This is not to exclude all such products, as those found in the supermarket such as Tylenol and aspirin (the latter a generic noun now, but a former brand name that still remains as such in Canada) are particularly relevant to the discussion. In practical terms, the type of brand name desired is one accessible in the broader speech community. Here the broader speech community refers to exposure of the brand name to a nation-wide group of speakers of English. Many of these brand names, however, go beyond that, having worldwide exposure, regardless of individual language boundaries. Such an exclusion as that made above does not however preclude the possibility of generic brand names in this category. The restriction is a necessary one, useful in setting parameters from which the overall study can develop.

Over the course of sifting through the INTA corpus, other eliminations will be made and the boundaries of inclusion will be further delineated. Similarly, in terms of the search for generic brand names one place to start is with the current and back issues of Editor & Publisher and Writer's Digest, both of which contain ads by companies attempting to protect their brand names from generic change (e.g., Kleenex > a kleenex). Yet, it is quite reasonable to argue that there would be no need to publish this type of ad if it were not for the fact that the name had already shifted to generic use.

Turning the discussion to the examination of brand names, I will first provide a listing of the types of relevant grammatical and semantic changes found in brand names. Many questions arise here regarding genericization. These questions include the following. Are certain semantic classes more easily changed to generics? Do any phonological considerations contribute to such change? What principles guide the change witnessed within the corpus? What factors contribute to a brand name becoming generic? Are the reasons for generic brand-name change simply linguistic (e.g., the need for a class term when one does not exist), or do social factors (e.g., market share, exclusivity in the market place) play a significant role in these changes? What factors in the creation of the brand name contribute to the change or lack of change in brand names? And finally, is genericization a regular process? It is therefore a goal of this book to answer these questions, which at present remain unexamined.

1.3 Overview

This volume consists of nine chapters. Each is discussed in detail below. Following this introduction, the second chapter will consist of an overview of research significant to this study. The literature review was one of the more difficult chapters to write because, rather than having a solid foundation of previous studies from which further research can be instigated, linguistically there has been little done. Therefore, it has been necessary to provide ample background into both the diachronic development of the brand and the research that has been conducted both on the brand name and upon linguistic change. This chapter has been divided into three sections. The initial section examines the historical development of both the brand name and of the legal development of

14

the proprietary status that brand names now possess. Continuing on, the second section offers background into the studies done on the brand name, both within and outside of linguistics. The studies in this section serve both as background on the brand name, but also frequently offer data collection methods applicable to this work, and which will be employed throughout this study. Finally, the third section considers relevant studies in semantic, and more broadly, linguistic change. The studies in this third section will pose theoretical questions that will be approached in the analysis section of this book.

The third chapter looks first at naming in general, and specifically at the place of names in linguistics. Then, it will be necessary to consider constraints placed upon names. This will serve to further narrow the scope of the study, yet at the same time will show why brand names are not what linguists have traditionally considered them to be (i.e., proper nouns). The discussion will therefore turn to the mechanics of the brand name, with specific reference to how this type of naming differs from other naming processes. Naming brands is a big business, and within business the techniques of naming are fairly well-known. This type of naming process runs in definite contrast to much of the arbitrary naming found in common nouns. Yet, these naming processes remain unknown to many linguists. Some of these techniques include the use of sound symbolism. Oaks (1997:192), for one, notes that 'Linguists have been aware of sound symbolism for many years ... But while this area of linguistics has represented an interesting curiosity within the field, it has not been given much serious attention.' The *Apple PowerBook* that I am currently writing this first chapter on was named through such a technique. As Cohen (1997:195) notes 'the p in Power supports compactness and speed, while the initial b in Book supports the perception of dependability.' We will look at sound symbolism in greater depth within this chapter. One of the more pervasive ways of naming a brand is through what Crystal (1994:388) calls 'deviant graphology'. This is simply 'purposeful misspelling' of the brand name (e.g., Wite-out) This will be significant to our discussion when we come later in the book to proprietary rights and language use concerning brand names. Other considerations will be deviation from standard morpheme boundaries (e.g., SnackWells), the use or disuse of capital letters, the importance of length in brand names, what makes a good brand name (Charmasson 1988; McCarthy 1987), and how some brand names are too good. Furthermore, as there are specific rules governing brand names these will be noted as well, insomuch as they are significant to the formulation of brand names. These include being formulated as a proper adjective followed by a common noun, that the proper adjective cannot be overly generic to begin with, and so forth. There is a great deal that can be said here about the nature of naming and how brand names are constructed and this has the potential to be a volume in and of itself. I will restrict my discussion to a single chapter.

Chapter 4 focuses on change in brand names and presents the hypotheses making up this theory of genericization. As no such research of this nature has been undertaken, this will provide a significant contribution to our understanding of the *hows* of brand-name change. Clearly part of this answer is a result of the general nature of language change. All languages (other than dead languages) are in a constant state of linguistic change. Yet, this only accounts for part of the answer and by examining **how** brand names change, through the application of my theory of generic change, we can begin to explain **why** some brand names become generic, and for the sake of the 'owners' of the brand name we can begin to suggest what can be done to avoid what the business community views as a negative consequence of brand naming, what I have named *genericization* and what the industry unjustly calls *genericide* (International Trademark Association 1993).[2]

Having accounted for the ways in which brand names change, in Chapter 5, the heart of this book, I will put forth four hypotheses to account for why brand names change. These will form my theory of genericization. Over the course of

---

[2] The predominant view of generic brand name change is death (>genocide) of the brand name, hence *genericide*. I take a rather different view of these brand names and consider them vibrant. *Genericide* contains an inherent bias that the alternative I propose, *genericization*, does not.

my first study of brand names, and a similar study recently undertaken (see Chapter 7 below) I have been able to formulate four primary observations that appear to hold true for brand names. These appear below.

> H1. If A is a brand name for an innovative product (one which did not exist before), then the association of that item with its name will become synonymous, rendering the brand name both a product name, and the name for the entire class.

> H2. If the predominant brand name in a semantic class(e.g., types of over-the-counter pain killers) is shorter than the corresponding class-noun, that predominant brand name will become the generic for the entire semantic class.

> H3. Ellipsis of the common noun is a prerequisite for generic brand-name change. The process is likely ellipsis of the common noun which in turn results in a grammatic shift from proper adjective to proper noun. The next step is proper noun to common noun. The common noun then may become a verb (when representing an action).

> H4. There must be a psychological association between a brand name and a single product. It appears that brand names which represent items from a number of different classes are much more difficult to attach a generic meaning to. For example, the brand name *Tylenol* can be attached to any over-the-counter pain reliever (excluding aspirin), and is only associated with that purpose. Compare that to *Chanel* which makes a multitude of different products (perfume, clothing, etc.). In other words, a generic meaning cannot be assigned because there is no single item association to be made.

It is expected in the examination of the corpus that additional generalizations can be made regarding generic brand-name change. While the presentation of the theory will be made in Chapter 5, Chapter 6 will consist of the actual analysis of the data collected in the corpus (Appendices A and B). A selection of tests will be run against each entry and the results will be tabulated and examined. What for example do the findings tell us about linguistic change in brand names, and specifically, generic change? One of the more problematic concerns of sociolinguistic studies of variation has been the question of actuation (Weinreich, Labov, and Herzog 1968), or how and why does variation begin? With the creation date of brand names known and through tracking change that brand names normally undergo, what can we surmise about broader linguistic variation and change as a result of this study? In other words, what can this study contribute to the long-standing problem of actuation?

Any unaccounted-for areas in the data will be noted in this chapter, as will any weaknesses in the method.

Chapter 7 consists of an examination of brand-name change and genericization in Japanese. This includes an examination of the principles of loanword change that have developed through the numerous studies on loanword borrowing into Japanese and other languages. Some attention is also given to native brands. For example, we recognize quite clearly that brand names from English, like all loanwords, will be modified phonetically to fit the syllabic structure and mora timing of Japanese, which destroys some consonant clusters, lengthens certain vowels, and creates phonetically long consonants (e.g., *tatta* 'built'). This section considers not only brand names borrowed into Japanese from English, but also to a limited extent will consider native Japanese brand names (their creation and organization) and the types of changes they undergo in order to determine whether there might be similar generalizations that can be made about how brand names change in Japanese. Theoretically, genericization should occur in Japanese just it does in many other languages. Therefore the first question is whether brand names borrowed into Japanese follow the same pattern as English. While expecting to find similarities to English (e.g., that genericization will occur in similar semantic classes as in English, and that the theory of genericization will be applicable cross-linguistically), one must recognize that there are some grammatical differences between Japanese and English. Beside the standard categories of noun, verb, and adjective, Japanese has adjectival nouns (such as *kirei da* 'pretty' which cannot take subject or object marking, yet which can take adjective marking *kirei-sa* 'prettiness') and verbal nouns (such as *setsumei* 'explanation' which require the dummy verb *suru* in predication *setsumei suru* 'to explain'; regular nouns cannot do this, **empitsu suru*). While one would not expect to find a brand name jumping categories to become an adjectival noun, one would expect a normal process allowing a shift from adjective to noun. *Bando eido* 'band aid' as in *Yubi kicchate, bando eido choodai* 'I cut my finger, give me a band aid please'. This is a good example because the American brand name *Band-Aid* (a proper adjective) was borrowed into Japanese and is being used as a noun (as it is in English), and furthermore can be used generically to refer to any type of small bandage. Yet the noun *band-aid* in Japanese has taken on far fewer senses than it has in English. Landau (1994:300-301) notes such additional senses as '... a *band aid* solution' and '*band aid* surgery' in English.

It should be likely also that one could find several brand names that have turned into verbal nouns. Shibatani (1991:217) notes *zerokkusu-suru* (<xerox) 'to photocopy' as one such instance. Note here the orthographic shift from the use of *x* to that of *z*. As Japanese is written much more closely to the way a word is pronounced, particularly in the writing of foreign words (using katakana), the use of the ze first syllable (cf. Japanese *zi* which is actually articulated as [ji]) is employed.

A second question is, how do borrowed brand names behave differently in Japanese? I have noted above that there are some basic grammatical differences between the open classes of English and Japanese. Are there certain pragmatic uses of brand names particular to Japanese? A further question is whether native brand names (those names created by Japanese companies for Japanese products) behave differently from those of foreign brand names and foreign products introduced to Japan? One native example that clearly comes to mind is *kuripu* 'Creap' coffee creamer, which is in frequent use as a generic noun representative of all brands of creamer in Japanese. Another example is *kinchooru* 'bug spray'

(<*Kinchoo*>) which is often used to refer to all bug spray similar to the way *Raid* is in English. While these all follow a pattern similar to those found in English, are there others that are different? Are there new unexpected senses applied to the brand that are not found in English? To offer an example from a different language, one meaning of *xerox* in Tagalog slang (other than as a photocopier) that has come into use is to describe a person who mimics another (Zorc and San Miguel 1991:127). What do such new senses tell us about brand-name change and how are these types of changes (changes in meaning other than from specific to generic) different from those of genericization?

Upon completion of the linguistic analysis of change in brand names in Japanese, it may be possible to make some generalizations about the influence of brand name upon the culture. Such examples as those above provide unique and interesting data. In terms of borrowed brand names which have infiltrated into Japanese, we may utilize some of the existing theory of the cultural reasons for borrowing-- status-raising and technological advancement (Shibatani 1991:149), name dropping (Tobin 1992), etc.-- yet the question that must be asked is, what significance does the use of the brand names make to the user? In considering this question, the work of James Stanlaw 1992 will be noted.

But what of the native brand names? Do they simply become generic as a result of market share alone, or for other reasons? Furthermore, how do social considerations dictate which brand names will be genericized?

The end goal of this chapter is a greater understanding of how brand names work in Japanese. The results will be considered in light of the results of the study of brand names in English.

Chapter 8 deals specifically with the issues and numerous complexities of proprietary law, language policy, and the brand name. Chapter 8 is intended to be most like the original study I completed on this subject (Clankie 1999) and is based loosely upon that study. In that study I looked at perceived misuse and at trademark education campaigns aimed at creative writers and editors. For this chapter it will be necessary to consider several questions. Namely, what does it mean to linguistic change when language is regulated by law? Can single lexical items be regulated effectively by law? These questions allude to the possibility that, to a greater extent, cultural and legal factors must be considered in order to adequately describe this type of linguistic change. Moreover, does the theory of genericization provide any answers to the business community as to how to better create a name that won't become generic? Finally, what does the fact that these names are regulated mean to linguistics? Proprietary law goes far beyond the narrow scope of this original study and has affected lexicographers and companies, and has become a major international issue. While the law is quite specific on the boundaries of trademark infringement, many companies have sought to extend the law far beyond its original intent (i.e., to protect one company's brand from another company). This runs contrary to the position of many people working in linguistics who have traditionally taken a functional view of language use and change (Aitchison 1981; Jennings 1981; and my own work). Linguistics, while having to consider prescriptivism, has tended to be a descriptive discipline. The present movement by business points to increasing restrictiveness and protectionism. This chapter will consider these issues and the impact that proprietary law has had on the use of brand names in both the written and spoken mediums. It will address the language mandates set forth in proprietary law and will also consider the efforts of the business community to monitor for perceived misuse. A point to be noted is that while companies attack others who 'misuse' the brand name,[3] they themselves frequently misuse their own names (most often using brand names as nouns in their own commercials). Here, as this is a discussion of language policy, discussions from language planning, namely the directionality of policy and whether a top-down (government-

---

[3] To these companies, any use of the brand name to refer to anything other than the product of that company is misuse. This includes any change in the grammatical category (e.g. from a proper adjective to a noun or verb), using the brand without the majuscule, and so on. Misuse here can also refer to different types of misuse, such as individual misuse vs. corporate misuse.

imposed) approach or a bottom-up (grassroots or population-instigated) approach, is more effective in influencing language policy will be relevant. Fishman 1991:395 has suggested a bottom-up approach to reversing language loss. While not directly relevant to the subject of brand name language policy, a by-product of such discussion is that in many cultures where a hierarchical structure of a traditional kingdom or of chiefs exists, where only top-down mandate has ever been realized, that a bottom-up approach may not be the most effective. If this is indeed the case, then the argument can be turned around. In democratic societies, where a strong bottom-up approach has always been in place, a significant amount of resentment towards prescriptivism, language police, language laws, and so forth in democratic societies will arise and the policy is destined to fail. In other words, the resentment comes as a result of what is perceived to be authoritarianism in light of democracy. This information is directly relevant to linguistic theory, as it could provide additional support for or against Fishman's approach and could assist in language planning efforts in other language communities. A broader examination of this and a number of other questions will be considered in this chapter.

The final chapter, Chapter 9, will wrap up what has been discovered over the course of this book and will begin with a summation of the findings. This will be followed by exposing some areas for further study as there will likely be a number of additional questions which will be raised over the course of the study.

A second concern here should be to answer the question posed early on as to what the findings tell us about why brand names change and what I as a linguist can discover about generic brand-name change that could serve as a resource to companies interested in creating brand names which are more resistant to change? The challenge to linguists is to demonstrate to companies that it is not the users of the language who have 'misused' the language, but rather it is the companies themselves who are responsible for generic brand-name change. Linguistic change is natural. What does it mean to misuse the language? Frequently the perspective from outside linguistics is decidedly prescriptive, with law and lobbying against perceived misuse being the most common response.

To conclude, this study is interested in the hows and whys of brand names, from their creation to the types of change they undergo, in an attempt to produce a theory to account for genericization which will be of interest to not only linguists, but also to companies that produce brand names.

In the next two chapters, I will discuss the background necessary for this study as well as an overview of naming processes. First, it will be important to begin with a discussion of the historical development of both the brand name and the laws governing this type of naming.

CHAPTER II. THE DEVELOPMENT AND STUDY OF BRAND NAMES

Perhaps your name is Rumpelstiltskin?
-The Brothers Grimm (Rumpelstiltskin, 1812).

This chapter is divided into three sections and will serve, along with Chapter 3, as a basis for the analysis to follow in Part II (Chapters 4-6). The first of these three sections in Chapter 2 examines the historical development of brand names from personal names. To fully understand this section, reference will be made to the legal statutes and foundations of the brand name in trademark theory and the shift in the focus of the statutes from protection of the public to protection of the company. Providing a foundation for the current structure and treatment of brand names, this first section will be followed by a brief examination of linguistic and other research on the brand name. This section can be broadly categorized by the type of research conducted and the intent of the work. These include works designed for proper brand name design, short pieces of entertainment value, studies of brand names in a given language, and those studies in linguistics which have touched upon the subject of brand names. Finally, in the third section I will examine significant studies in semantic change and universals relevant to this study. These will include research on types of semantic change, semantic primitives, the motivations for semantic change, and the actuation of semantic, and more broadly, linguistic change.

2.1 Historical Development of the Brand Name

The historical record regarding brand names is a rather sketchy one. Room 1987:13 traces the origin of the brand back at least as far as the Greeks and Romans. He points out, 'Much early advertising and marketing (in the literal sense) was thus done on a personal basis with the name of a particular individual as important as that of his product or service. The modern development of this can be seen in the name of the private shopkeeper over his shop and some of the best known chain store names have originated as that of a single shop named after the original owner.' It is not a great stretch to see the link between personal names and the later development of the brand name in its proprietary sense, the latter developing as a result of the former. *J.C. Penney's* (<James Cash Penney), *Sears* (<Richard Warren Sears), and *Macy's* (<Rowland Hussey Macy) demonstrate the personal name as a proprietary name. In practical terms, the original brand name was likely to have been the name of the maker of that item. Kuwayama 1973:6 also dates the earliest brand marking to the Greeks, potters' marks found on pottery in the Corinth area, dating back at least 4,000 years. From the early potters' marks found in Greece, little is known of the actual spread of branding to other parts of Europe, and in other parts of the world, or whether branding simply sprung up in a number of different places as the need arose. Apart from the Corinth pottery, which today remains the oldest pieces bearing some form of branding, the historical record is vague with some later items of Greek and Italian pottery dated to the fourth and fifth centuries B.C. also said to be bearing pottery makers' marks (Schecter 1925:20), but there is little else for examination.

I have discussed at some length now the origins of the brand. The question that should now be considered is whether any evidence exists of linguistic change of the brand in the historical record, in other words, some evidence of generic brand-name change. In Schecter's work one very striking example was noted. In Schecter 1925:168, he refers to the British case in the English Court of Appeals of Corona cigars. He writes,

In that case the owners of the "Corona" cigar brand sought to enjoin the delivery of cigars of other brands in response to requests for "a Corona." Defendant, whose defence was financed by the large cigar manufacturing interests of Havana, while admitting the validity of the "Corona" trade-mark and conceding plaintiff's title to that mark, claimed that in the course of time "Corona" had come to mean in the public mind not merely a brand but also -- and to a greater extent -- a size and shape of cigar. The Court of Appeals would appear to have based its decision sustaining plaintiff's right to an injunction on the ground that the trial court had found as a fact that to the *majority* of the public, "Corona" still meant a brand and not merely a size or shape of cigar (Havana Cigar & Tobacco Factories, Ld. v. Oddenino, 1923, 41 Rep. Pat. Cas. 47, 56).

Deducing the process of generic brand-name change, Schecter 1925:168-69 continues, "... the reasoning of the Court would imply that if a sufficient number of infringers were able to becloud in the public mind, 'Corona' would thereby become a size or shape and would cease to be a brand ..." This is in effect the procedure the courts have taken to identify if a brand name has entered the common domain. It is worth noting here that Corona, while still a popular brand of cigars, shows no evidence of remaining a generic brand name. In other words, one does not ask for *a box of Coronas* meaning anything other than the brand Corona. It is not equal to asking for *a box of stogies*, which one could use to refer to any of a number of brands of cigars.

With a limited amount of information available about brand names historically, a misconception regarding the regulation of brand names (as one form of trademark) has developed. A common practice in the legal profession throughout this century has been to consider trademark law to be a product of the industrialization occurring in the nineteenth century. Room (1987:14) for example states, 'Modern branding and the use of individual brand names has its origin in the nineteenth century.' Opposing this narrow view, Schecter (1925:11) remarks,

Nevertheless, those who have attained pre-eminence either as practitioners or as text-writers of trade-mark law have with few exceptions been quite content to regard that law as practically the creation of the nineteenth century, without attempting in any way to ascertain the extent to which trade-marks had been used prior to the nineteenth century, the functions or purposes which these trade-marks had served and the methods, if any, by which they came under any form of legal protection or surveillance.

Despite the dating of Schecter's remark and the clarity with which the evidence points to the trademark and some rudimentary form of trademark law existing many centuries earlier, the view shared by Room and others continues today.

From data available through the vast legal records of the British court system, Schecter 1925 has compiled perhaps the most complete search identifying court statutes regarding the history of the trademark, the earliest evidence of which dates to the reign of Henry III in 1266 concerning the marking of bread. The *Statutum de Pistoribus* dictates that 'every baker shall have a mark of his own for each sort of bread' (Schecter translation of *Quilibet Pistor habeat suum proprium signum super quodlibet genus panum suorum*). Schecter has identified statutes for goldsmiths, clothiers, weavers, wax-workers and others dating also to the Middle Ages.

It is important to note at this point the importance of the association between the visual image and the written word or mark. This brings us to three important dichotomies; first the subject of visual vs. written forms, secondarily orality (e.g., singing, recitation, and memorization (Havelock 1986:21), vs. literacy (the ability to read and write), and third the oral form of the word in English vs. its written form. Each of these three dichotomies are of particular importance, and all are interrelated. Room (1987:13) remarks that during this period[4] (presumably the middle ages onward) the use of the visual image arose

---

[4] Room does not specify the period to which he is referring, although one can infer that he is referring to the Middle Ages.

out of necessity, as much of the buying public was still illiterate. The picture was then the main way by which many people could identify the purpose of the business. What does this fact, that there had to be an association between the visual image and the written word, have to do with the historical development of the brand name? To answer this question, it is this amalgamation of the visual image with the written word which remains today on many signs for businesses, on product packages, and through other forms of advertising. Some of these symbols are systematic (uniform) in nature (e.g., the green cross on pharmacies throughout France), while others are individualistic, showing the particular characterization of the business or product by the owner or designer (See for example, pub signs in Britain). Historically, we can view the linking of the image to the word as a transitional move toward literacy. Yet, this should not be viewed as a move away from orality. Rather, this tradition takes place in addition to an oral tradition, not an abandonment of one method for another, as both continue today. A similar development to that in England occurred much earlier in Greece, with the move from orality to literacy as exhibited in Homer's *Iliad* and *Odyssey* and Hesiod's *Theogony* and *Works and Days*, the earliest works in written Greek, appearing in the 7th Century B.C. (Havelock 1986:19). In both the English and the Greek examples we are looking at a process, one that has continued through time. The difference however, is that in the Greek case the move was not from an <u>illiterate</u> to <u>literate</u> society, but rather from a <u>non-literate</u> society (i.e., with no written language), to a <u>literate</u> one. In the realm of business affairs during the Middle Ages however, this linking of visual and written forms represented a move by those who were literate to attract the business of those who were illiterate, hence the linking of the picture to the written word. As it is the written form that will be important to this study, it should be noted that frequently it is only through the written word that we can account for what is happening in the oral language (See for example Havelock's (1986:21-22) treatment of Euripides <u>Hippolytus</u>), as

28

often the cues to a change in progress may be most readily manifested in evidence found in the written language. In brand names, this means for example, demajisculization as a marker of genericization. As Ong (1982:175) points out:

> Orality is not an ideal, and never was. To approach it positively is not to advocate it as a permanant state for any culture. Literacy opens possibilities to the word and to human existence unimaginable without writing.

It is the permanancy of the written word over the spoken language, a point Ong is alluding to here, that drew me to focus primarily upon the written aspects of genericization. Once this study of the process of genericization in a written corpus is complete, it will then be possible to work to a greater extent than is possible now on the spoken aspects of generic change.

Yet, there remains another issue, that of further differences in the oral form and the written form. Taking for example, the brand name *xerox*, written phonetically as /ziraks/, we can see that the written form does not closely match the way the form is articulated. English permits a great level of flexibility in the spelling of the written form of the word. In contrast, the Japanese hiragana and katakana syllabaries restrict the orthographic representation more closely to the sound represented by the closest syllable in the syllabary. For example, the sound /te/ has only one hiragana and one katakana character. To elaborate, in Japanese when a word is written, particularly a foreign word, it is written in katakana according to the way it is articulated in speech (at least as closely as the language permits). The example of *xerox* --> *zerokkusu* in Section 1.3 demonstrated this point[5].

Returning now to the legal background of brand naming, while Schecter was capable of identifying statutes to the thirteenth century, the earliest known

---

[5] The exception to this is with the kanji characters, which in many cases, offer a range of possible characters for a particular sound, the variation depending solely on the meaning(s) of each character.

example of a court trial involving a trademark was not found prior to the seventeenth century, in the case of Southern vs. How in 1618 (reported in 1656). In that case, involving the infringement of a clothier's mark by the maker of an inferior version of the same, the report states,

> Doderidge (sic) said, that 22 Eliz. the action upon the case was brought in the Common Pleas by a clothier, that whereas he had gained great reputation for his making of his cloth by reason whereof he had great utterance to his benefit and profit, and that he used to set his mark on his cloth whereby it should be known to be his cloth: and another clothier, observing it, used the same mark to his ill-made cloth on purpose to deceive him, and it was resolved that the action did well lie (Popham's Reports, 1656 in Schecter, 1925:7).

Schecter notes however, that while the legal precedent was set with Southern vs. How, cases of trademark infringement must have existed prior. Yet, as many of professions of this period involved self-regulating guilds whereby disputes were arbitrated within the guild, taking one's case to the courts was prohibited. This would then account for the abrupt lack of court evidence between the earliest known statutes and the earliest recorded legal contest of those statutes.

Schecter (1925:9) highlights the significance of the precedent set by Southern vs. How and the 'considerable weight as authority for the proposition that the unauthorized use of a trade-mark is unlawful and may be the subject of an action in deceit.' Southern vs. How is the essence of modern trademark law as it exists at present.

From Southern vs. How onward, early trademark statutes faced a major theoretical quandary concerning the purpose of the trademark. The quandary centered upon whether the purpose of the mark was to protect the public against fraud, or whether it was to protect the owner of the trademark against damage created as a result of someone else using the mark (proprietary right). The records clearly point out that the early concern favored protection of the public. This runs in direct opposition to current trademark practice, which has done little more than turn the brand name into property, favoring the owner of the trademark. Protection of the public has been relegated to a minor secondary concern. Schecter tracks this shift to a 1923 U.S. Supreme Court decision, overturning an earlier appeals court decision requiring proof of deception of the public. In this case (A. Bourjois & Co. v. Katzel 260 U.S. 689), the Supreme Court required no such proof, while only highlighting the damage to the owner of the trademark. (Schecter 1925:6). This decision, while shifting the purpose of the trademark to protection of the owner, also led to a subsequent clarification of who may or may not use the trademark. In an decision made a few months later (Prestonettes, Inc., v. Coty 264 U.S. 359, 368) and on behalf of the court, Mr. Justice Holmes writes,

> Then what new rights does the trademark confer? It does not confer the right to prohibit the use of the word or words. It is not copyright ... A trade-mark only gives the right to prohibit the use of it so far as to protect the owner's good-will against the sale of another's product as his...When the mark is used in the way that does not deceive the public, we see no such sanctity in the word as to prevent its being used to tell the truth. It is not taboo (Schecter 1925:155).

While granting the significant capital expenditure involved in the creation and maintenance of the brand, the court clearly recognized the danger involved in granting proprietary rights to language and that some form of boundary was required to prevent the overextension of the proprietary domain to something akin to copyright of the word. It will be apparent in Chapter 8 however that many companies believe they possess absolute right to the brand name, essentially cornering and restricting its use.

This first section has set out to provide a historical and legal framework from which it is possible to see the diachronic development of the brand name, and the shift in focus of trademark law to a proprietary entity. If we turn now to the origin of U.S. trademark law as it relates to protection, the earliest records show that the trademark was a concern as early as 1788 involving the production and sale of sail cloth. The statute, approved in 1789 states,

> That all goods which may be manufactured by the said Corporation, shall have a label of lead affixed to the one end thereof, which shall have the same impression with the seal of the said Corporation and that if any person shall knowingly use a like seal or label with that used by said Corporation, with a view of vending or disposing thereof, every person so offending shall forfeit and pay treble the value of such goods, to be used for and recovered for the use of the said Corporation, by action of debt, in any court of record proper to try the same (Act of the General Court of Massachusetts, February 3, 1789 in Schecter, 1925:131).

Though it is apparent that trademark law existed in some form from the earliest days of the United States, much of trademark theory as existing in the eighteenth century was a product of English law, brought intact from England, almost certainly during the period of British rule during the seventeenth and eighteenth Centuries. The same theoretical problem of the purpose of trademark law existed, and as noted above, it was in the United States that the shift to protection of the 'owner' of the brand name first occurred.

With some insight now into the historical development of the brand as one form of trademark, and the legal development with respect to the theoretical underpinnings of the law both in England and the United States and the inherent relationship between the two, a final question arises. When speaking of branding one cannot talk for long without at least considering the connection to the branding of animals. The question then, is, to what extent are brand names connected with the branding of animals? In both cases, one is placing a distinguishing mark upon the 'product' to differentiate it from that of another producer. However, while potters' marks to 4,000 B.C. have remained a part of the historical record, the evidence of branding in animals, or more specifically, the simple process of burning one's mark into an item (not only to animals, but also to inanimate objects such as woodburning) is far less clear. Yet, turning first to the etymological evidence of the word in the OED may offer some clues to this relationship. The word brand (originally *brond(e)*) referred to 'burning' or 'fire' with the earliest evidence from Beowolf (a1000:4258) 'Hy hine ne moston .. bronde forbaernan'. The first reference however to the branding of animals appears in the later part of the seventeenth century. The example, from 1667, is as follows, 'For yr brand of horses they shal have ye letter V on ye near buttock'.[6]

While possible to connect the branding or marking of animals to the seventeenth century, the process of burning one's mark most certainly must go back farther into history. Noting earlier in this section that the Statutum de Pistoribus in 1266 regulated the marking of bread, the question that must then be considered is how the marking of bread was undertaken? Schecter 1925 offers a broad discussion of the marking of bread over two centuries, but fails to explain how the marking was accomplished. Was it in the form of a mold used to impress a mark in the bread as it rose? Or was it a dye-based mark pressed onto the bread (as sometimes occurs on Chinese *bau*)? The third possibility however, and one that would seem entirely plausible, is that the mark was burned into the bread. However the evidence remains unclear. The actual text from the Statutum de Pistoribus provides little evidence to further this possibility, '*Quilibet Pistor habeat suum proprium signum super quodlibet genus panum suorum*'. The word applied here for the mark was not *brond(e)*, but rather *signum*.

If we pause for a moment to consider the connection between the word *brand* and the trade-mark, the OED lists the earliest use in this sense as 1827, 'The proprietors have added the brand mark 'Margam' on each box.' This marking process was also likely to have been as a result of burning, as noted in the sense given in the definition (OED 1989 V2:488), 'A trade-mark, whether made by

---

[6] An earlier example is noted from 1665 "They shal enter such saile..in the said brand booke". It is a far less apparent example however, when decontextualized, than the 1667 example. Therefore, for the purposes of presenting clearer evidence, the 1667 example was selected. The 'brand booke' mentioned in the 1665 example appears to be a register of brand names, probably maker names for the particular sails.

burning or otherwise (Applied to trade-marks on casks of wines or liquors, timber, metals, and any description of goods except textile fabrics.)'

With a historical understanding of the brand, we can now turn to the second portion of this chapter, namely the linguistic and other research previously conducted on the brand name.

2.2 Linguistic Studies of the Brand Name

The study of the brand name in linguistics has been seriously lacking. Of the studies that have been done, there has been no prevailing theoretical pattern from which to work. Each study simply existed in isolation, a very small piece, frequently noting some quirk, or that generic brand-name change was occurring. No study has made a significant effort to explain why this change occurs. With this in mind, one can look at the studies that have been done, in order to demonstrate the significant amount of opportunity existing within the underexamined area.

Despite the proliferation of the brand name throughout the language, brand names have been largely overlooked. No more than a handful of serious studies exist. Among these are Vanden Bergh et al. 1984, Lederer 1985, Lentine and Shuy 1990, Cohen 1998.

Vanden Bergh et al. 1984 examined phonetic traits of brand name recall and recognition. They hypothesized that an initial plosive in a brand name and short word length would result in greater recall and recognition. Using computer-generated nonsense words proposed as potential brand names, Vanden Bergh devised a mixed sample of words beginning with and without plosives. In their results, they found that in a survey of 300+ students, words beginning with plosives were more frequently recalled and recognized than those beginning with other consonants or beginning with vowels. A secondary finding of this study was the correlation between recall and recognition and the length of the brand name (i.e., the shorter the name, the easier it is to remember). Vanden Bergh et al. found that monosyllabic brand names were recalled more frequently than trisyllabic forms. Results for monosyllabic and disyllablic forms were insignificant. Both of these findings will be of greater importance again in the theoretical discussion to follow in Chapters 6 and 8 of contributing factors which facilitate brand-name change.

Phonetic considerations of the brand name, and in particular, how the brand name is constructed, or is to be constructed, have created a small niche market for linguists as consultants for companies on brand name design. Cohen 1998 in a summary of his company's (Lexicon Naming) research noted the following concerning the subject of sound symbolism, or the relationship between sound and meaning or perceived meaning. In a pilot study of 144 students, students were surveyed for possible names of three hypothetical products (a performance sedan, a laptop computer, and a headache tablet). The results of Cohen's study appear below.

Voiceless stops (p, t, k) carry a greater connotation of speed than do voiced stops (b, d, g). Eg., Pavil sounds faster that Bavil.

Voiceless stops (p, k) connote smallness better than voiced stops (b, g). E.g., Kortan seems smaller than Gortan.

Fricatives (v, f, z, s) connote speed better than stops (b, p, d, t). E.g., Sarrant seems faster than Tarrant.

Z connotes smallness better than s. E.g., Zyndron seems more compact than Syndron.

Voiced fricatives (v and z) connote speed better than voiceless fricatives (f and s). E.g., Valdon seems faster than Faldon.

Dentals (d and t) connote speed better than labials (b and p). E.g., Taza seems faster than Paza.

Stops (b, p, d) connote dependability better than fricatives (v, f, z, s). E.g., Bazia seems more dependable than Vazia.

D seems relatively dependable, while g seems relatively
undependable. E.g., Damza seems more dependable than Gamza
(Cohen, 1998:194).

It is unclear from Cohen's work, however, whether these findings are
exclusive to English, or whether they may be applicable across languages. It is
likely however, that at least some forms of sound symbolism would be found
universally in language, for example in the vowels where a long vowel may
represent length or exaggeration.

Turning now from the perceptual effects resonating from a class of
consonants, to semantic considerations, Lentine and Shuy 1990 studied the *Mc-*
prefix (as in McDonald's), suggesting that the *Mc-* prefix is now a generic
morpheme possessing a meaning of 'basic, convenient, inexpensive, standardized'
(354). In their study, a study solicited as testimony in the trademark infringement
case of Quality Inns vs. McDonald's, in which Quality Inns sought to create a
chain of hotels called *McSleep*, Lentine and Shuy surveyed the Nexis media
clipping system for all words containing the *Mc-* prefix for the period of March to
July 1988. The goal of the work was to come to some understanding of how
speakers and writers use the *Mc-* prefix. In the 94 tokens used in the study,
Lentine and Shuy found the prefix to be productive, applicable to a wide variety
of products and services (what I will be calling semantic classes). Notably, they
isolated seven separate senses or functions and each token was then organized
into the appropriate category.

1. Ethnic Associations (including surnames)
2. Alliterative patternings arising from a proper name
3. Acronyms
4. Products of the McDonald's Corporation
5. Macintosh computer products or related businesses
6. Parodies of a fast food product or service
7. The meaning 'basic, convenient, inexpensive, standardized'.

Significant to this current study, 56 tokens were classified into the last category (7) and the one of relevance to the trademark infringement suit. Lentine and Shuy had successfully demonstrated the lack of inherent relationship or specificity of the *Mc-* prefix to the McDonald's Corporation, as those in category seven bore only the graphic similarity to the word *McDonald's*. When attached to a lexical item of a differing semantic class, the *Mc-* prefix bore little relationship to the McDonald's fast food chain, and any perceived relationship would continue to decline rapidly. This suggests the vibrance with which the Mc- prefix is spreading within the language, carrying the senses of meaning which may have originated with McDonald's, but which have moved away from that association while retaining the qualities of inexpensive convenience. Furthermore, they noted the importance of context to determine the possible sense attached to the lexical item.

The simplicity of the method of the Lentine and Shuy study and their analysis lend themselves quite well to this study and will resurface in a modified form in the building of the corpus in Chapter 5.

The study above demonstrates that generic brand-name change is not exclusive to the entire name alone, but rather that a productive morpheme such as *Mc-* (McDonald's, McRib, McShake, etc.) can also take on additional senses and can undergo the process of genericization.

As this discussion moves toward the heart of this study, several of what may be called 'after-the-fact studies' are worth noting. In these studies, the author may note the fact that this form of change is occurring and frequently lists brand names that have become generic, or which are perceived to be moving towards genericization. While many of these studies are quick to note the influence of commercialism upon language, they are often lacking in substance, produced more for their entertainment value than their linguistic contribution. Lederer 1985, Tankard 1975, Adams 1987, Baron 1989 and others fit into this category.

There are also lay articles, often those geared to educating the public of the 'appropriate' use of the brand name. Like the articles of the preceding paragraph, these articles, while created for a purpose other than linguistic inquiry of a scientific nature, offer a level of validation that a given set of brand names is indeed generic. The simple fact that they are being talked about in the context of generic class terms suggests a broadening of senses beyond the brand alone. Studies such as Finn 1995, Terez 1994, and others fit into this category.

On occasion, generic brand-name change is mentioned in passing by linguists conducting research in areas of language change, and in general linguistics texts. Bolinger 1980:65-66, Cruse 1986:146, and Crystal 1994:388 show the awareness of linguists of the fact that advertising has an impact on the language. Yet, this remains an area of little interest to many linguists.

Turning now to studies on brand names other than those in English, one study worth noting here is Chan and Huang 1997. In their study, aptly titled *Brand Naming in China: A Linguistic Approach*, Chan and Huang challenged the Eurocentric tradition of brand naming, stressing the importance of the individual linguistic market over universals in brand naming. Their corpus-based study of 527 'award winning' brand names took into account phonetic, morphological, and semantic considerations and found a number of interesting results. First, the phonetic concerns consisted of syllable structure and tone structure.[7] Chan and Huang found the preferred syllable structure (brand length) for Chinese was two syllables. 90.5% of the tokens were made up of this pattern. This was followed by brand names that were trisyllabic with 6.45%. Contrary to many western marketing texts which suggest the shorter the brand name the better it will do, monosyllabic brand names in Chinese only accounted for 2.1% of the most successful brand names surveyed.

For tone structure, the preferred tonal pattern was high-high. This pattern accounted for 47.13% of the 157 disyllabic brand names. This was followed by a low-high pattern at 25.48%.

---

[7] Syllable structure here, as Chan and Huang use the term, alludes to the length of the brand name in syllables, and not the traditional notion of syllable structure in linguistics (i.e. CV, CVC, etc.).

The most successful semantic connotations for effective brand names in China were those which reflected a positive connotation (66.03), or neutral connotation (33.78).

In examining the morphological structure of Chinese brand names, Chan and Huang noted 14 different compounding strategies and found that the most commonly occurring strategy was that of a noun-noun compound, arising in 51.61% of the brand names surveyed. This was followed by adjective-noun combinations at 10.06%. A number of other possibilities were also employed, but those made up an insignificant percentage in the results.

To summarize their findings, Chan and Huang 1997:233 on the basis of linguistic evidence found that the combination of factors that would offer the greatest chance of a successful brand name was a two-syllable word with a high-high tone pattern, positive connotations, and a noun-noun morphemic structure.

It is worth noting here that Chan and Huang wrote this particular article not for linguists but rather for marketing planners. It is encouraging to see linguistic considerations in the private sector. Chan and Huang fail to note however, any evidence that any of these 527 successful brand names have broadened into a generic brand. Two such studies which do however mention (in passing) generic brand names in a language other than English are both on Japanese, by Stanlaw 1992:66 and Shibatani 1991:217. Stanlaw mentions generic brand names in the context of a discussion of advertising language in Japanese. Shibatani on the other hand, was referring to the ease with which Japanese readily accepts and adapts foreign words into the language. In both of these studies, the generic brand names mentioned are those based upon loanwords from western languages (mainly English). No mention was made of generic brand names native to Japanese. In Chapter 7 however, I will note several found in my own work on Japanese, adding to the variety of languages for which this phenomenon has been reported.

Perhaps the most influential work on the brand name in linguistics is that done not by a linguist, but rather by the psychologist Monroe Friedman 1985,

1986, 1986b, 1991, who has been particularly influential to my work on brand names, and is perhaps the most widely disseminated writer of scholarly work on the brand name.[8] In a collection of studies on hit plays, newspapers, and novels Friedman repeatedly found an increase in brand name usage over twenty to thirty year periods. It would be redundant to reiterate the reference to these studies made in Section 1.1.1, and further mention will be made to these as necessary.

As is apparent above, the study of brand names to this point has resulted in an eclectic mix of studies that are only vaguely tied together by the fact that they study brand names. Below is a selection of studies on linguistic change, and more specifically on semantic change.

2.3 Relevant Studies on Semantic Change

In this last section, it is important to identify relevant studies of linguistic change which may aid in our understanding of genericization. The subject of semantic change in linguistics has been a tempestuous one. As McMahon (1994: 175) writes, 'Are there regular semantic changes, with recurring types; or must we accept that 'every word has its own history'?' She notes that among the primary obstacles to studying semantic change is its linking of meaning with culture. On this point she writes, 'This means that to understand a change in meaning we may also require a good grasp of the socio-cultural situation within a speech community ...(175).' The linking of meaning to culture here is an important one. If we are to come to some understanding of the process that motivates generic brand-name change we must have some understanding of the cultural background which may create the appropriate circumstances for the change to occur.

---

[8] I have deliberately cited Friedman's work as linguistic research, despite Friedman's background in psychology. It is the historical association between psychology and linguistics (with Chomsky for a time viewing linguistics as a branch of psychology), and the very nature of Friedman's writing, that warrant his inclusion into this section on linguistic studies of the brand name.

What is it about words that makes semantic change so prevalent? McMahon identifies three aspects of meaning that permit semantic change. First, she identifies the polysemic nature of words. Most words contain more than one meaning. This is necessary, as she points out, because words are used in a variety of contexts by different speakers, who may or may not share the same intended meaning for the word.

The second motivation for semantic change McMahon identifies is that 'language is transmitted discontinuously (177).' She writes,

> Children do not receive a fully-formed grammar from their parents, but create one for themselves on the basis of incoming data (with, in the Chomskyan theory, some help from innate constructs). Children may therefore learn imperfectly, or make abductive inferences which alter the language.[9]

Finally, McMahon (177) points out that semantic change is possible because of what Saussure called 'arbitrariness of the linguistic sign'. As McMahon explains, the sign (word) is 'bipartite', consisting of a signifier (a string of letters or sounds) and something signified (the meaning). The point made about arbitrariness of the sign is that the signifier and signified are arbitrarily linked. There is no reason, for example, why the word *sea* should refer to a type of large body of water and not a dish or an animal. By isolating the signifier from the meaning, McMahon writes, the two can change independent of one another.

While the first two motivating factors commented on by McMahon are quite applicable, the third is problematic. Widely known in linguistics are cases that are non-arbitrary. Onomatopoeic expressions are frequently cited, and McMahon acknowledges this. She argues however that onomatopoeic expressions are generally very stable. In direct contrast, lexical items with an arbitrary relationship between sound and meaning are more apt to change. Thus,

---

[9] McMahon fails to specify to which of Chomsky's theories she is referring.

it appears that the arbitrariness of the sign would indeed be a contributing factor to the facilitation of semantic change. Yet, there are other types of non-arbitrary lexical items and, as was mentioned earlier in this chapter, Cohen's work on sound symbolism contains a mesh of sound and meaning much less arbitrary than the exclusivity suggested by the Saussurean principle. In Chapter 3, this will be approached in greater detail, as many naming processes are anything but arbitrary. Do these types of non-arbitrary lexical items share the same resistance to semantic change? As brand names are very intentionally created, the sounds carefully picked, the perceived senses of the name scrutinized, these names are frequently found changing semantically. A broader discussion of this very point will continue in the next chapter.

Some further mention must be made in this context of Bloomfield 1933. For the purposes of this study, the form of semantic change exhibited in genericization is semantic widening, or broadening. To reiterate from Chapter 1, semantic widening occurs when a given lexical item takes on new or extended senses. In the case of the generic brand name the new sense will be a generic class representation *Wite Out* > *wite out* or *white out* (meaning 'correction fluid'). In many cases, one of the newly created senses will gain prominence and will become primary. The original meaning may then be relegated to a minor sense.

While not in direct comparison to semantic change, some mention must also be made to universal semantic primitives. In this volume, much discussion will center upon the notion of the semantic class term, the common class-noun which is said to attach to the proper adjective in the creation of a fully-formed brand name. The class-noun differentiates the product or service from similar yet different products and services. Furthermore, we must consider cross-linguistic applicability of the theory of genericization and of class-nouns, in other words, a level of universality where the existence of the capitalistic notion of the brand name presupposes a similar existence of genericization. If this is indeed the case, then to what extent can we define the class-noun across languages? Here I believe it is possible to draw upon the work of Goddard and Wierzbicka 1994 and others on semantic primitives. Amidst the list devised by Wierzbicka and others, is the primitive *kind of*. *Kind of* is said to mark meaningful taxonomies and we can draw upon it as the semantic primitive for what I will be calling class terms in this work.

2.3.1 The Causes of Semantic Change

Meillet 1912 identified three causes for semantic change. These were linguistic, historical, and social reasons. McMahon 1994:180 provides an excellent explanation of each of these. The first type, linguistic factors, is exclusive of external causes. She notes grammaticalization as one type of linguistically conditioned change.

Historical causes for semantic change include technological advancement. The meaning frequently changes with modernization, while the form of the words remains unchanged.

Social causes for semantic change occur when a new meaning develops from use by a particular group or when a word used with a particular sense by a given group gains broader acceptance within the community (McMahon 1994:180). Broader acceptance here suggests a change moving through the community.

In addition to these, Ullman 1962 presents a fourth: psychological causes. This may include taboo forms, euphemism, and as McMahon suggests, reinterpretation by the child.

Grace 1993:685-686 takes a different approach to language change. In his work, Grace postulates a hypothesis regarding one's knowledge of language (KOL) that is behind language change. Grace states,

Individuals' knowledge of language is nothing more than a large
memory store of experiences--with the emphasis on experiences in which
language was used. For linguistic purposes, we may think of this as
essentially a store of utterances. We interpret what's said by recalling
other cases where the same thing or something similar was said. We
decide what to say by recalling similar situations and what was said in
them (and what the consequences were).

In a later study (Grace 1997b:1) he summarizes, '... the reality behind
language states, and therefore linguistic change, turns out ultimately to be
individuals' knowledge of language (KOL).' This leads us to the subject of the
actuation of these changes.

2.3.2 Actuation of Language Change

The problem of how linguistic changes begin, or the actuation of linguistic
change, has been a longstanding one first highlighted by Weinreich, Labov, and
Herzog 1968. On this, they write the following:

The over-all process of linguistic change may involve stimuli and
constraints both from society and from the structure of language. The
difficulty of the actuation riddle is evident from the number of factors
which influence change: it is likely that all explanations to be advanced in
the near future will be after the fact (186).

Since writing the above statement in 1968, actuation has remained a
theoretical problem today. Little significant progress has been made in explaining
how linguistic change begins. It is hoped that at the end of this study something
may be said in addressing this concern. The advantage of studying brand names
is that each brand name has a visible recorded date of creation. And this is how
brand names differ from other types of lexical item for which no actuation date is
known. It is hoped that this study will be able to contribute further to addressing

the problem of actuation. Such findings will be discussed in greater detail at the end of Chapter 6.

2.4 Conclusions

This chapter has taken into account three divergent concerns. The first was the historical development of the brand name from personal names to product names and eventually to proprietary status. To show this progression it was necessary to present some legal grounding of the court cases which played a direct role in the development of the brand name in British, then American society. As the focus of this study is primarily English this portion of the chapter is decidedly Eurocentric. Evidence from non-European countries however, may show unanticipated differences, and is an area warranting further study.

The second part of this chapter was a general literature review of the scant work done on the brand name. It has included work from outside linguistics that is of relevance to this study, discussion of how brand-name change is generally treated, and work that has considered linguistic theory. Several of the studies have offered direction in empirical data collection on brand names applicable to this present study (Friedman 1985, 1986, 1991), and to study techniques replicable in my own work (Lentine and Shuy 1990).

The final section of this chapter looked at studies of linguistic and semantic change relevant to the study of brand names.

In Chapter 3, the discussion will turn to the mechanics of name creation beginning with other forms of naming practice, then will examine the construction of brand names and how they are grammatically different from other forms of naming devices.

CHAPTER III. NAMING PROCESSES

The master's right of giving names goes so far that it is permissible to look upon language itself as the expression of the power of the masters.
-Friederich Nietzsche, (1887) On the Genealogy of Morals

This chapter, like Chapter 2, will be divided into three parts and will consider the vast subject of naming processes. The first section will consider the place of names in linguistics. The second section will examine whether names are constrained by particular languages, free of constraints, or alternatively, are both constrained and unconstrained. Finally, the last section of this chapter will discuss the mechanics of brand name creation, and how naming brands differs from other types of naming process.

3.1 The Place of Names in Linguistic Research

Within linguistics, the study of names (onomastics) and the significance of the power of naming have been largely taken for granted. Nouns for example, clearly make up the largest of the open classes in English. If we take the lay definition of a noun to be 'a word that is the name of a person, place, thing, quality, action, etc., and can be used as the subject or object of a verb' (Longman Dictionary of Contemporary English 1983:460) we begin to get a sense of the

46

immense productivity found within naming.[10]   I suspect there are very few
linguists who are familiar with onomastics within linguistics, yet we should all
recognize the contributions of onomastic study to broader linguistic issues. As
Nuessel (1992:5) notes, 'the study of names relates directly to at least three
academic endeavors: formal linguistics, the philosophy of language, and
ethnography. Despite the interdisciplinary nature of onomastics, the study of
names has remained at the periphery of formal linguistic theory ...'

As linguistics students we are often indirectly taught the importance of
naming practices. We fail however, in many cases, to recognize them as such.
Studies of kinship terminology teach us how particular cultures construct their
own realities. Yet, if these studies of kinship do represent the construction of
reality in individual cultures, is it not as a result of the evidence found in the
names used to address kin? Similarly, we are made aware (often wrongly so) of
the number of terms for snow in Eskimo (Boas 1911; Whorf 1940) as a means of
demonstrating differences in perception placed on items by their importance to
that particular culture. While this particular example has been shown to be
nothing more than a myth (see for example Martin 1986 and Pullum 1991), other
examples, such as the number of camel-related expressions, show the importance
of those animals in countries where they play a central role in life.

Folk taxonomies, or the ways individual cultures classify entities, are also
widely taught in the broader tradition of linguistic anthropology. As Frake (1962,
reprinted in 1969:28) points out, 'an ethnographer should strive to define objects
according to the conceptual system of the people he is studying.' The importance
of folk taxonomies then was to determine the classification system as utilized
within a particular culture, not to try to apply our own system of classification on
another culture. Such taxonomies also set out to identify the meaningful contrasts
made within a culture for distinguishing items. This is demonstrated in such

---

[10] Of course nouns might also be described in terms of form or distributional criteria. O'Grady
(1996:3) writes that nouns 'denote individuatable things, and can co-occur with deictic
determiners and other markers of individuation.'

studies as Frake's earlier 1961 study of disease diagnosis among the Subanun of the Philippines. This particular area, the area of folk taxonomy, will be important to keep in mind when we enter the broader discussion of the class names and the created classes of brand names (Chapters 5 and 6), many of which are generated entirely within the business and legal communities, but which have a direct impact on the language as a whole.

As students, we rarely approach studies such as those noted above in terms of the simple fact that we are talking about naming. Naming is, however, quite important to mainstream linguistics and is being approached in its own right to a greater extent by scholars. One recent doctoral dissertation worth noting is Piller 1996 which focuses on the construction of American automobile names (see also Aronoff's 1998:658 review of Piller).

It is of course possible to distinguish within the broader category of names between common names and proper names. Pulgram 1954:42-43 distinguishes proper nouns (names) from common nouns as below.

1. Names
   a. Only in the singular
   b. Without determiner
   c. Always definite
   d. Species of object contains only one specimen, but
      (1) Name may be preceded by connecting it with a determiner: two Johns, a Macintosh,
      (2) Name may be preceded by the definite article: The Mississippi.
2. Common Nouns
   a. In singular and plural
   b. With determiner
   c. Definite and indefinite
   d. Species of object occurring in more than one specimen.

Within the broader class of proper names, several domains of names have been examined. One domain is the study of placenames (toponyms), which have long been of interest to historical linguists, cultural anthropologists, and others.

These names for example, may be the only evidence available on extinct languages (e.g., Celtic, Gaulish), or on earlier stages of a particular language. Basso (1990:106) in studying Western Apache placenames remarks, "... placenames are intricate little creations and (that) studying their internal structure, together with the functions they serve in spoken conversation, can lead the ethnographer to any number of useful discoveries." Bender 1970 in his study of Marshallese place names summarized and identified several important roles and uses played by place names in linguistics.

1. 'testimony of extinct languages' (Bloomfield 1933:464)
2. as evidence for reconstruction of earlier languages and forms
3. for the identification changes in linguistic frontiers
4. potential reconstruction of proto-forms of known cognate names cross-linguistically
5. for insights into the naming process
6. indicating the types of constructions making up place names
7. identification of the parts of speech making up place names
8. the grammatical properties of the names
9. which patterns are favored cross-linguistically (6-9 from Hockett 1958:303, 311-12).
10. the correct recording of their names at present
11. analysis of their meanings
12. analysis of recurrent forms which no longer bear meaning
13. ethnological analyses (folk taxonomies, etc.)

The information provided by place names is certainly greater than it would at first appear. Others have worked on distinct taxonomies of naming such as plant names, animal names, and so forth. Much of this work has originated in linguistic anthropology, and with a small group of onomastic scholars.

Yet, there are also other forms of naming in proper nouns. These include acronyms (NASA, HUD), anthroponyms (personal names), and eponyms (the Heimlich maneuver < Dr. Henry Heimlich), pseudonyms, anagrams, pen names, stage names, and many more. And to this, the brand name makes up an additional category of naming. While little has been done on these types of names within linguistics, outside of linguistics historical work has been done for example on the etymologies of family names by historians, genealogists, social psychologists, and others (Smith-Bannister 1997; Ashley 1989).[11]

Early on, students of linguistics are taught of Saussure's 'arbitrariness of the sign'--that there is, as Salzmann (1993:22) puts it, 'no intrinsic relationship between the form of a meaningful unit of a language (for example, a word) and the concept for which the unit stands.' What we call *bird* in English, is *tori* in Japanese, *oiseau* in French, and so on. Rather few linguists however have gone on to consider how much meaning there is in proper names, brand names and the like, and the care that is taken in choosing what is perceived to be 'the right name'. If I name a rottweiler Brutus, is it not because Brutus has some sense of strength attached to it? Setting aside contrast-naming (e.g., naming a chihuahua Zeus) which sets out to accentuate an opposing characteristic, I certainly would not name a rottweiler Fifi, even if it were a female. Many children in American society are named after biblical characters, and others after movie stars. Are Lucy, Gomer, and Gilligan truly arbitrary? Certainly not anymore in American English. There are even annual surveys done of the most popular names for babies, and most people are aware of names that seem out-of-date. Carroll (1985:163) goes so far as saying '... the claim that names are perfectly arbitrary contradicts the thrust of empirical research ... names are not arbitrary.' There is considerable debate in onomastic research regarding whether proper names connote meaning as other words do, or denote it, and whether the arbitrariness of the sign can be fully extended to proper names.[12] Jespersen 1965 has argued that proper names are rich in connotation, even more so than common nouns. This is

---

[11] It is interesting to note that in nearly every introductory textbook of linguistics names are given at least nominal coverage (see for example Lehman 1983 or Akmajian et al. 1990), yet it seems that names are for the most part treated as a linguistic novelty rather than as an area for serious study.

[12] For further discussion see Nuessel 1992:2 versus Carroll 1985:163.

certainly an area where much more research needs to be done, as the ramifications for such a finding would most certainly be of great interest to linguistics.

Names translated across languages frequently run into problems as with the case of the *Chevy Nova*, where in Spanish the *no va* was interpreted by Spanish speakers to mean 'It doesn't go.' Cross-linguistically something gets added or lost in the translation. While *Coke* remains 'Coke' across languages, its former slogan 'Coke brings good things to life.' in Chinese came out 'Coke brings your ancestors back from the dead.' To this extent the study of names in translation is important. Unlike common nouns, rarely do brand names get translated across languages, and when they do it is of interest to the linguist to understand why they had to be translated, and in what ways they are altered.

Lexicographers have often had to consider issues of naming, particularly in relation to what names and what types of names are to be included in a dictionary. These may include but are not limited to proper names, homophonous forms, trademarks, and company names.

Similarly, linguists have often been interested in discussions of metalanguage, the words we use when we talk about language. This may range from the rather benign discussions of grammatical categories, or may be extended to the discussions of how different cultures name their language (e.g., whether they have a word for their own language per se, or whether they express it with the same word they use for the tribal name, or by some other means).

Inevitably, names extend into many aspects of life. They should be considered in terms of not only their place in linguistics alone, but also as a focus of interdisciplinary study. In fact, while onomastics is often overlooked, naming should be viewed as present in much of linguistics, particularly those branches interested in issues of performance. This would then include not only those groups of linguists mentioned above, but also in the branches of pragmatics (for how people choose to name things and the uses of names), linguistic anthropology (for the classifications applied by individual cultures, and naming ceremonies), historical linguistics (for what names tell us about earlier forms of a language), semantics (for the meanings attached to names) and so on. The study of names need not be restricted to issues of use alone. The more traditional components of linguistics may have some interest in naming as well. Morphologists may be interested in how names are constructed, grammarians in what counts as a name and what constructions allow names, and phonologists in areas such as sound symbolism and the interface of sound and meaning in names. Some of the most fundamental of linguistic studies by Saussure, Whorf, and Jesperson have dealt with naming concerns. Names provide a vast wealth of information about history, change, and meaning. It would be quite difficult to pin down a precise branch of linguistics where names could not offer insight.

While it should now be clearly evident that names play an important, yet somewhat undervalued, role in linguistic study, I now turn to whether names are in some sense specific-language bound, or whether names are free of language constraints, or possibly a combination of both.

3.2 Constraints on Naming

In examining the constraints placed upon naming, it will be necessary first to consider universal versus language-specific tendencies of naming. From there, the broader discussion of constraints will take shape.

3.2.1 Potential Universals of Naming

In the study of names, several potential universals have surfaced. The search for universals is important, in so much as 'their description may shed considerable light on the nature of the human language facility' (Brown 1984:8). To begin, according to Kaplan and Bernays (1997:16) 'Names are ... cultural universals. Apparently there has never been a society able to get along without them.' Here Kaplan and Bernays are referring to personal names given to people, and while they do appear to be universals, surnames are not (Hughes 1961:7). As Alford (1987:1) reports, 'In all societies, individuals typically receive a name or a set of names, and in no society are names applied unsystematically or randomly. The bestowal of names follows more or less explicit rules in every society.' An appropriate starting point here is the purpose of naming. In a very broad sense, naming is a universal phenomenon of language. All languages must have some form of naming, as reference and identification are among the most primary of functions in language. Yet, the ways in which individual cultures choose to name and organize things, the folk taxonomies, are often very individualistic. This is evident once again in the example mentioned earlier of the many camel-related lexical items found in languages where camels play an important role in life. Contrasting that with America, where the closest many people come to a camel is Joe Camel, we have at best the distinction between one-hump and two-hump camels. Linguistic taboos in naming are also individualistic. Often, there is a direct preference in many cultures for the use of kinship terms over real names. In other cases, name changes are called for in cases of sickness, accidents, or death.

Similarly, names may be given according to the partrilineal line, matrilineal line, both in the surnames (if available) and in the given names. The names may also be given (as with many Native American names) in accordance with traits in nature.

If we narrow this discussion down, naming serves several purposes. The first is as a referential function. That is, people name things to be able to refer to them. Philosophical arguments abound regarding a theory of proper names (Russell 1956; Frege 1970; and most recently Fitch 1987). It is likely that reference was quite important in the development of language in humans.

A second purpose is for differentiation. Differentiation here refers to the distinguishing of one entity from another.

Another apparent universal is found in the way that people tend to name certain domains. Berlin and Kay 1969 in their widely cited study of color terms found that in the languages surveyed (98 in total) there was a particular ordering of color, a hierarchy of color throughout language. Berlin and Kay found that all languages distinguish at least light and dark. If they have a third color name, it will be red. The fourth and fifth color names are interchangeable, either green or yellow. Blue is then the sixth color name. It is important to point out here that these 'basic' color terms are actually naming points on the spectrum. While an apparent universal in terms of the patterning of cultural world view, the number of colors a given language may have is clearly individualistic. While the arbitrariness of names given to colors (e.g., *blue* in English, *aoi* in Japanese) is often exclusive to each language, such study provides cognitive information which may be quite informative to understanding the processes involved in, and which govern, naming.

The most thought-provoking finding of Berlin's earlier work (1973) was his generalizations regarding classification and taxonomies. These have been characterized by Brown (1984:3-4), who states the following, 'these generalizations indicate that humans everywhere use essentially the same strategies in organizing knowledge of biological phenomena.' Brown goes on to note that 'cross-language regularities have been reported for the domains of body-part terms, personality concepts, geometric-figure terms, and adjectives--to mention only a few.'

Cross-cultural studies such as Berlin and Kay 1969 and Alford 1988 suggest that researchers believe that there are both similar constraints and processes involved in naming and individual differences which are language-specific. From the selection of studies presented above, it is evident that names are both bound by constraints governing their creation and uses, and free to a considerable extent in their taxonomic classifications, based upon the construction of reality in individual cultures.

Continuing this discussion, it is useful to look the ways in which names might be constrained in specific languages.

3.2.2 Ways in which Names might be considered Specific-Language Bound

It is perhaps best to look at the ways in which names might be considered specific-language-bound. One way of approaching this is to think of the constraints languages may place on names. Syntagmatic restrictions are placed upon names. Excluding for a moment brand names, names generally function as nouns. As such there are constraints on what can appear in front of a name or after it. Common nouns are preceded by an article in English, proper nouns generally appear without an article, and so forth. Other languages, such as Japanese, will mark common nouns and proper nouns not by articles but rather by the inclusion or exclusion of a title marker (*-san*, etc., in proper nouns such as personal names). With that exception, both forms of names are marked by their grammatical function alone in Japanese.

Similarly, names are bound by the phonotactic constraints of a given language. Starting a name in English with a velar nasal would be problematic because English only permits velar nasals in the coda of a syllable, and most native English speakers would be culturally or linguistically incapable of saying it. Asking a native speaker of English to read aloud names such as Nguyen, or Nkrumah, demonstrates this point. This is not to say that one cannot violate the phonotactic constraints in the construction of a name, but that under normal circumstances people simply don't. So in this sense, clearly phonotactic constraints of a given language will bind the naming process.

While the linguistic constraints on names are rather straightforward, there are a number of social constraints individual languages bestow upon names. This involves the rather intricate matter of what to say, when, by whom, and how it is to be said. Let us take for example the constraints placed upon personal names in English. With the exception of a limited set of unisex names (of which *Shawn* is one), personal names distinguish males from females. We know for example that in English *Mary, Susan,* and *Julie* are female names, and *Charles,*[13] *Peter,* and *Fred* are names for males. We are here constrained in what we are permitted to name a baby. Violating the social rules of naming (naming a little girl *Herman* for example) would violate these social constraints and would likely alienate both the parents and child. Yet, it is perhaps through some violation of these constraints (much less severe than the previous example) that over time some of these names do become unisex names.

The differentiation of male and female is only one of the social constraints placed upon names. In many languages names carry distinct meanings, and are created to connote such. Japanese is one such language. There the government regulates what one can name a child. If the Japanese *kanji* characters selected by the parents are too archaic, difficult to read or write, or if the characters carry some form of negative innuendo, the local government may refuse to allow the name to be registered on the family register (*koseki*). To offer a classic name for discussion, my wife's name is *Mikiko*. It has three *kanji* characters each one representing a mora (and in this case a syllable also). The meaning of the characters can be translated as 'child of the beautiful century' or alternatively as 'beautiful child of the century'. While most names conform to the social rules for naming children (i.e., the name should be pleasant, modern, etc.) there are people who are challenging the norms of what is culturally acceptable to name a child. A now famous case in Japan is the man who tried to register his baby boy's name as *Akuma*. *Akuma* is a common noun which means 'devil'. The man appealed to the courts that he should be able to name his child whatever he chooses. The courts disagreed. Clearly, there are societal norms in place on acceptability. While in the United States it is not unusual to find people with names which push societal norms *Moon Unit Zappa* or *River Phoenix,* or even those which are plays on words such as *Pete Moss,* current major league baseball player *Mike Colangelo,*

---

[13] Charlie, or Charley however, can also be used for females. Charles itself, however, is a male name.

and my favorite *Ima June Bugg* (the latter found in Ashley, 1989:71), it is likely that there would be a significant amount of societal angst about someone naming their child *Satan*.

A current constraint on naming can be found in what is allowed to be put on vanity license plates. Many state governments (Illinois is one example) keep a list of lexical forms deemed offensive or suggestively so, restricting the names that can be placed on these vanity plates.

In some cultures, certain names are considered taboo to the common classes. This tends to be a widespread phenomenon in domains such as the names of one's parents, names of the dead, chiefs, or of religious and spiritual leaders for example. In the latter two cases (chiefs and religious figures) the resulting reference would be through title alone.

Another important factor is that the taxonomies placed on naming items in individual languages is highly indicative of their perceptions of the world. Recalling the Sapir-Whorf Hypothesis[14] (Hoijer 1954) there are two points of concern. The first is that language influences the way we think about things, known as linguistic determinism; and the second is that differences among languages will be reflective of differences in world views. While agreeing that to a large extent today the language that we use predisposes us to thinking about the classifications of things in a certain way, it is much more likely that the connection between language and perception of reality is reciprocal, feeding on one another. Language likely arose out of a need to identify and to make reference to certain entities (as well as a need to communicate and to warn of danger). In this sense, early on, certain taxonomies were developed. Through time these taxonomies were reinforced within the speakers of the language, at the same time new taxonomies were continuously arising, with old ones disappearing. While the general principle that language reinforces our perceptions is likely, this

---

[14] Hoijer (1954) suggests that the foundations of what came to be known as the Sapir-Whorf Hypothesis are Sapir (1929 reprinted in Mandelbaum 1949 and 1931:578) and Whorf (1952:5).

principle is somewhat limiting. I would like to consider these taxonomies as reflective of collective thought in a culture and that such taxonomies are bound in specific languages. It is not surprising, for example, that in English we separate hair, feathers, and fur into separate lexical items, as they are perceived as different from one another, but in Thai they all are accounted for in a single lexical term. This suggests that to a speaker of Thai these are actually similar in some respect.

It may seem now that what Whorf is suggesting is in violation of what Berlin and Kay 1969 found regarding color terms, and other perceived universals of naming. At a more abstract level however, universals are not contradictory to Whorf. Individual cultures will often distinguish colors in different ways, despite following a universal in the hierarchical arrangement of colors. Some cultures such as the Hanunoo for example, will distinguish 'wet green' from 'dry green', whereas English doesn't (Conklin 1964:191)

The study of plant names is also informative in discerning how different groups name plants. In English for example, newly discovered plants are given a scientific name based upon the family from which the new variety descends, and a common name which is frequently comprised, at least in part, of the name of the finder. Commercial varieties of flowers and new hybrids contrastively, are given names like *Midnight's Passion* (a good name for a rose) as descriptive of its believed qualities and to promote some kind of judgment value on the flower. In other cultures such as on Pohnpei, plant names may be named after the finder, or, in the case of a hybrid, the creator.[15]

3.2.3 Ways in which Names are Free of Constraints

As shown above, names tend to be highly structured entities governed both by universal tendencies in their purpose and to some extent in their

---

[15] An excellent source of studies conducted on folk taxonomies can be found in Conklin's (1980) *Folk Classification*, a bibliography of references to 1971.

classification of real world entities. Now it is possible to turn the discussion to ways in which names may be conceived as being free of constraints. As noted at length earlier, the arbitrariness of the sign only carries so far. In common nouns it is quite accurate. We are free in a language to name an un-named entity what we like, so long as it does not violate the language-specific norms of the society. Yet, in naming people, where we are naming new entities with old names, there stands to reason that these names are no longer meaningless strings of phonemes. Forms of names such as proper names and brand names are much more highly constrained, as they are frequently regulated by societal norms, and increasingly by government norms. Of brand names Ashley (1989:178) notes, 'Brand names are arguably the most painstakingly chosen names of all in our society. Almost all names try to impress us or project an image ...[16]'

It is however possible to point out ways that names can be considered free of constraints. Creativity in naming is one such way. There are no finite limits on the number of names in any domain that we may have or even that a single item can have. Similarly, we are free to create new names as needed and to create new names for old things. The system is quite productive. Names are free to change structurally, phonologically, and semantically, or simply to disappear from the language. Language changes over time. Names, both common and proper, will change as well.

In regard to the constraints on naming, I would like to suggest that while common names for items are rather free of constraints, proper names of various kinds and proper adjectives are highly constrained by linguistic and cultural constraints in many cultures. This is not to say that they are totally constrained, as it is possible to identify cultures where the birth of a baby for example, requires the creation of an entirely novel name. The search for a theory of naming then, would suggest that there are constraints governing all names, and that the freedom

---

[16] While this may be true, many parents would argue that selecting the name of one's children is no less painstaking.

in the choice of a name exists in the differences placed on naming processes by each individual culture.

A variety of naming processes have been discussed in the previous sections of this chapter. Now, turning the discussion to the subject of brand names, it will soon be evident that the creation, structure, and motivations in brand naming differ in a number of ways from other naming processes.

3.3 The Mechanics of Brand Naming

The search for the perfect brand name is a complex one. Creating the perfect name has become a big business in and of itself, with a number of consulting firms specializing in that sole task. Numerous books are available to aid in the selection of a good brand name. In the remaining portion of this chapter, I will first examine a number of elements involved in the creation of brand names. If we can come to some understanding of the practice of brand naming, both the psychological rationale for attempts to create a successful name and the legal constraints upon naming which result in the clear naming patterns present in brand naming, this information will then serve as evidence of why such practices contribute to the changing of the brand to a generic. Once this background has been established, consideration will then be given to the differences between brand names and the types of names covered in sections 3.1 and 3.2.

To begin this discussion of how brand names are constructed, it is important first to consider the constraints placed by the law upon those who create brand names.

60

3.3.1 Legal Constraints on the Brand Name

United States trademark law (i.e., Lanham Act of 1946, Trademark Revision Law of 1988, and Federal Trademark Dilution Act of 1995) recognizes four distinct types of brand name, each type possessing a given level of protection by the law. These appear as follows.

1. Fanciful or coined marks (which generally have the broadest protection): These are words that are made up and have no built-in meaning (*Kodak* for cameras and *Exxon* for petroleum products).

2. Arbitrary marks: These are existing words with no relation to the goods or services (*Apple* for computers and *Tide* for detergent).

3. Suggestive marks: These are words which suggest some attribute of or benefit from the goods or services, but do not describe the goods themselves (*Coppertone* for tanning lotion, *Caterpillar* for tractors, *Whirlpool* for washers)

4. Descriptive marks (which generally have the narrowest protection): These describe the goods, services or a characteristic of them. They cannot be protected until they have achieved distinctiveness through use and advertising, which is called acquiring 'secondary meaning' (*Car-freshener* for an auto deodorizer, *Rich 'n Chips* for chocolate chip cookies and *Homemakers* for housekeeping services). Included within this group are laudatory words (such as *Gold Medal* for flour and *Blue Ribbon* for beer), geographically descriptive terms that truly suggest an association with a place(*Bank of Texas* for a Texas bank's services), and surnames (*Gallo* for wines). (Borchard, 1995:4).[17]

---

[17] My use of italics of the mentioned brand names.

To summarize the categories above, novel brand names in the language are granted the most protection under trademark law. Arbitrary names, where an existing word is applied to a product or service bearing no relationship to the actual product, is next. Suggestive marks, those brands containing a quality of the product or benefit, are protected, but less so than the more arbitrary forms. Finally, descriptive marks are required to generate a secondary meaning prior to registration, the secondary meaning creating distinctiveness in that semantic class. This type of brand name, because of the relationship and shared meaning between the brand and its semantic class, holds the least protection under the law. It would seem rational that if generic change were to occur, it would occur in those brands that shared meaning (either partially or in full) with the semantic class to which that brand belongs.

3.3.2 Formation of the Brand Name

In examining the mechanics of brand name creation it is possible to identify a number of strategies that are employed to create a viable brand name. Charmasson 1988:83ff reports on nine types of brand name formation. It should be noted here that many of these strategies are based on the written form of the brand. The importance of the written form of the brand should be stressed here, particularly since one of the major factors in determining generic use in writing is the loss of the majuscule, or capital letter. As this study is based upon a written corpus, matters of orthography cannot be overlooked. Each of these strategies will be examined briefly.

The first strategy employed in constructing a brand name is simply to select an existing lexical item from the language, such as one for an unrelated object, and to apply it as the name for the product. Identifiable examples of this are *Apple* for computers, *Agree* for shampoo, and *Ace* for bandages.

If a single lexical item cannot be found for the product or company name, a second process, that of joining two or more complete lexical items may be employed. This is a process known as *composition*. *KitchenAid* home appliances, *SnackWells* pastry snacks, and *DoveBar* ice cream confections offer examples of this type of name construction. Note the disregard for morpheme boundaries and the overuse of majuscule letters in these names as distinguishing features in the written form from common nouns.[18]

A third formation strategy is through *fusion*, or blending. This process involves two lexical items and the overlapping of one or more of the letters in the two words. *Foamaster* (<foam+master) a defoaming product, *ReaLime* (<real+lime) lime juice, *Totaline* (<total+line) air conditioner parts, and *Selectric* (<select+electric) typewriters all demonstrate this process.

Tacking or *derivation* is a process by which a prefix or suffix is added to an existing lexical item to create a novel form. *Mailgram* (<mail+-gram) message delivery services, *Autoharp* (<auto-+harp) musical instruments, and *Permapaper* (<perma-+paper) recording paper typify this type of naming process.

Clipping is another technique for producing a brand. This process shortens existing lexical items, frequently deleting syllables, to produce a novel form which still contains the shading in meaning of the original full form of the word. *Fanta* (<Fantastic) soda pop and *Pan Am* (<Pan American) airways model this naming strategy.

A further type of naming process Charmasson includes is a category consisting of two types; first, purposeful misspellings of existing lexical items, and second, the addition of an extra letter or two. The first type of alteration is found in brands such as *Holsum* (cf. wholesome) bread, *Mello Yello* (cf. mellow yellow) soda pop, and *Day-Glo* (cf. day glow), which typify purposeful misspellings. Examples of the second category--brand names adding additional

---

[18] Following the orthographic rules of the language, we should have *Kitchen Aid* or *Kitchenaid*, but not *KitchenAid*. Yet, it is precisely this type of variation that makes the brand name stand out.

letters--include *Milka* (<milk) chocolate, *Steak-Umm* (<steak) sandwich steaks, and *Regaine* (<regain) hair-growth treatment.

Analogy, as in other areas of language, is a very productive way of producing new brand names. Traditionally in linguistics analogies are four-part problems, where three parts are known and the fourth is inferred (e.g., *drive* --> *drove, dive* --> *dove*). If we consider analogy in the lay sense (two-part problems), then brand names said to have been formed by analogy include *Laundromat* (<Automat) self service laundries, and *Empirin* (<aspirin) aspirin.

There is also the *portmanteau* (Hockett 1947), or blend, is a process where elements from two or more lexical items are combined to form a new word. Often cited examples in English include *brunch* (<breakfast+lunch), *motel* (<motor+hotel), and so forth. In terms of brand names employing this strategy, one popular one while I was growing up was *Broasted* chicken (<broiled+roasted), a process of cooking chicken that sounded quite appetizing but which in reality was little more than pressurized deep-fat frying. Other examples in brands include the *Cran*+fruit combinations (*Cranapple, Cranicot*, etc.), and *Funyuns* (<fun+onions) onion flavored snacks.

Charmasson identifies *ideophones* as a further strategy for the construction of brand names. This process includes sound symbolism as presented in Chapter 2. In linguistics, these are generally called *phonesthemes* (Householder 1946: 83). Blust 1988:4 views the phonestheme as falling into an intermediate category between a phoneme (the minimal meaningless unit of structure) and a morpheme (the minimal meaningful unit of structure), with a distinct sound-meaning association. Ideophones then, employing the Blust treatment, are phonesthemes which produce a suggestive meaning. To offer an example, whereas liquids and sibilants can be used to portray softness (silky), the *sl-* combination in *slick, slide*, and so forth suggest as Charmasson notes, 'a gliding or sliding movement' (91). Cohen 1998: 193ff mentions *Clorox* and *Chanel*, where the obstruents in *Clorox*

(/k/ and /s/) suggest masculinity, and the sonorants in *Chanel* (/a/, /n/, /l/) suggest femininity.[19]

The final category Charmasson identifies is what he calls *multimedia names*. These are simply combinations of two or more of the above mentioned techniques. The example above of *Funyuns* includes not only a blend based upon *fun+onions*, but also includes an alternative spelling (ions --> yuns) to distinguish the name and can also be considered a multimedia name.

As is evident, there are a number of strategies available to those who create brand names. Room 1982:15-16 offers six criteria for a successful trade name. These are presented below.

(1a) Visual comprehension
(1b) Pronounceability in most languages
(1c) Avoidance of objectionable or absurd meanings.
(1d) Positive references.
(1e) Ease of recall.
(1f) Conformity to legal prerequisites for official
      registration.

While 1b, 'pronounceability in most languages' would seem to be a difficult task to seek to accomplish in a single name (given that the most recent estimates place the number of languages somewhere in excess of 6,000), Room is suggesting that a number of factors play a role in the ultimate success of a brand name.

This section has sought to present a brief examination of the considerations present in brand naming from a marketing perspective. It is notable that little concern is made for linguistic research or how these strategies and traits contribute to genericization. In the next section, I will look at how the brand name differs from other types of naming process.

---

[19] For further discussion of phonestemes and sound symbolism see Jakobson and Waugh 1979 (Chapter 4), Tsur 1987, and Hinton et. al. 1994.

3.4 The Brand Name vs. Other Types of Name

As has been alluded to over the course of the first three chapters, brand names are distinct in several noticeable ways. To begin, the date at which the brand name entered the marketplace and, as a result, the language, is easily identifiable. One can discover, for example, that the brand name *Coca-Cola* originated in 1886. It is this capacity for precision that allows for a more exact tracking of the brand name diachronically than other types of names. How do we, for example, date the name *John*? The OED lists the earliest form of *John* (Hebrew *yohanan*) with no clear date. The earliest reference to *John* in English (*Iohannes*) was not until the twelfth century. Did it exist prior to the Hebrew entry? And what of common nouns? For identifiable inventions we may have a date, but what of naturally occurring phenomena? Certainly the etymologies aid greatly in trying to answer these questions. Historical reconstructions may also identify, or aid in identifying, proto-forms of the word. The difference here is the precise certainty of the information available on brand names, much of which history has deleted from other types of name. Furthermore, as the vast majority of brand names in English originated at the end of the nineteenth century and throughout the twentieth century (with the rise of capitalism), this area of naming remains unexplored.

A second identifiable difference can be seen in that brand names frequently violate many of the rules of the language. As mentioned earlier, deviations in the spellings and morpheme boundaries of existing lexical items frequently produce combinations not seen in other parts of the language.

A further difference noted throughout the first chapters of this study is simply that brand names carry a proprietary status allowing for protection under the law. Other types of name are not normally afforded this status. The use of personal names for example can not be restricted in the same way. One can not stop another person from using the name *Fred* as a personal name. An exception to this is applying a well-known person's name to a product for which that person has no vested interest or knowledge. I could not for example name my new brand of motor oil after President Bill Clinton. I could, however, name a child William Jefferson Clinton Clankie if I so desired. One should not construe from this discussion however, that a personal name cannot be a brand name. Many brand names historically originated from personal names. These are the dual-function trade names mentioned in Chapter 1. *Macy's* is only one such example.[20]

Finally, as most names are grammatically nouns (either proper or common), brand names are legally proper adjectives. While this may seems unlikely, it is actually a development out of legal practice. In an effort to isolate the brand name as marking the origin of the product rather than the product itself, all brand names are required by law to be used alongside a common (class) noun. This has resulted in the brand name being relegated to the position of a proper adjective, as in *Xerox* photocopiers. This is a particularly compelling strategy as it attempts to remove the use of the brand name as either a proper or common noun, yet it is a double-sided one. Legally, the trademark is a proper adjective. However, if we view the common noun as a functional zero, in actuality when they enter the community they are proper nouns. And this is generally how the public views them. While creating proper adjectives is not a particularly strong defense against genericization, it does create an extra change in the process of genericization. The main problem of this regulation however, is that few consumers know that brand names are legally proper adjectives. The assumption that most people make is that these are simply proper nouns, and hence, they become proper nouns through usage.

---

[20] In some cases, we do find change going in the opposite direction, that is, away from the family name. The Hawaiian department store *Liberty House*, was changed from *Hackfeld* (a family name) during World War I because the family name was thought to have been 'too German'.

3.5 Conclusions to Chapters 1, 2, and 3

In Part I of this study I have sought to establish a solid background of linguistic and nonlinguistic research into; (1) the history of the brand name and (2) treatments of the brand name within and outside of linguistics. Chapter 1 introduced and defined the brand name and trademark, and provided an overview of the issues to be dealt with in this study.

Chapter 2 presented a historical examination of the development of the brand name out of the personal name. This chapter also considered the historical foundations of trademark law, showing that the original intent of the law was not so much as a proprietary tool, but rather as a means of protecting unwary consumers against fraud.

In the present chapter, I have examined several types of naming processes. I began by examining the role of names in linguistics, the constraints on names in language, and whether any identifiable universal strategies exist. This was followed by a description of the mechanics of brand names creation. Finally, I looked at the differences between brand names and other types of naming processes.

Part II provides the core of this study, made up of the theory of genericization (Chapter 4), testing of the theory (Chapter 5), and analysis (Chapter 6). I now turn to the formal presentation of the theory of genericization.

PART II: THEORY AND ANALYSIS

Chapter IV. A Theory of Generic Brand Name Change

Science is nothing more than a refinement of everyday thinking.
-Albert Einstein, (1936) Physics and Reality

Before proceeding to the theory of genericization that is at the heart of this work, it is important to consider the types of change that a brand name can undergo. If we can come to some understanding of how a brand name changes, we can then begin to address (1) the problem of why some brand names become generic, and (2) the contributing factors for such change. This chapter will focus on open-category grammatical changes originating from the proper adjective, and the semantic changes that make up broadening. Both types of change can be seen as central to the theory.

In the second section of this chapter, I propose a pattern in brand name change. It is predicted that there is a regular, identifiable pattern of generic change. As neither the specific grammatical changes involved in semantic broadening nor the subject of patterning has been addressed in previous studies on brand names, this information will provide a new foundation from which one can get a clearer view of genericization and the mechanisms for genericization to take place.

Section 4.3 presents in greater depth the hypotheses that make up this theory. Each hypothesis will be treated individually, beginning with its rationale.

This discussion leads into Section 4.4, which focuses on the construction of the corpus of 100 generic brand names that will be tested and the procedures involved in the selection or elimination of certain generic brands from the corpus. This section also challenges the corpus, considering any weaknesses present in the construction design, and examines both the testing of the hypotheses and how the tests might disprove the hypotheses. In other words, what counterevidence would be necessary to falsify the hypotheses?

To begin this chapter, the grammatical and semantic changes involved in genericization are considered.

4.1 Generic Changes in Brand Names

4.1.1 Grammatical Changes

Proper Adjective --> Proper Noun

The first type of change undergone by brand names, and by far the most prevalent, is the change in grammatical category from a proper adjective to a proper noun. As has been noted in earlier chapters, all brand names in English are constructed as proper adjectives followed by a common class noun (e.g., *Jell-O* gelatin). It is through ellipsis of the common noun that the proper adjective changes to a proper noun. Ellipsis is very common in English. As McMahon (1994:184) explains, 'ellipsis results from the habitual contiguity of two forms; one ultimately drops, and the leftover form stands for the whole string.' She notes several examples with common-noun phrases including *private* (soldier), *to win a gold* (medal), and a *daily* (paper). Brand names, as two-part phrases, adhere to McMahon's definition. What was, for example, *Jell-O* gelatin then became acceptable as simply *Jell-O* (and later jello).

At this point I am setting aside the semantic shift from specific to generic, as many non-generic brand names undergo this same change (e.g., *I bought some*

Miller (beer) for the party tonight or *He smoked a Swisher Sweet (cigar) on his way to work*).

Proper Noun --> Common Noun

It is the second type of change, the shift from a proper noun that is capitalized and representative of a specific product, to a common noun in lower case, that is dictated by the semantic shift in meaning from specific to generic. *Coke* to *coke*, *Saran Wrap* to *saran wrap*, and *Kleenex* to *kleenex* demonstrate the significance of this step in genericization. The loss of the majuscule in spelling is in line with the association of the name as the class term, and frequently the loss of association with the brand. This extension of the meaning of the brand name to include any similar product of the same design results in many cases from the name being learned as a common noun, not as a brand name. In my own ideolect it is possible to identify several brands that I had never recognized as such, having learned them as the name of the item, never making the association to the brand, and now learning of their status as brand names. *Plexiglas*, *Fiberglas*, and *SheetRock* are a few from the area of construction materials. This type of change will be demonstrated in greater detail in the next two chapters.

Common Noun --> Verb

The third type of grammatical change involving brand names is the change from a common noun to a verb. *To xerox* (something), *to rollerblade, to mace* (someone), *to scotch guard* (something) all demonstrate the productivity of this type of change. Here too there is little association between the brand and the common action verb resulting from the change. One could be using any similar product with the same purpose and these verbs would be fully applicable.

This type of change is also frequent outside of brand names, occurring often in English. *A stone* and *to stone someone* are one case, as in *I threw a stone* and *He was stoned to death for his beliefs*. *Work* and *to* work, *a dance* and *to dance*, and *a fight* and *to fight* demonstrate the productivity in this particular process. The question that is likely to arise to the perceptive reader at this point is the relationship between the productivity of the noun-to-verb changes evident in the common-noun examples above and what I have identified here as the common-noun-to-verb changes found in brand names. As the change from proper adjective to verb is of limited productivity in the rest of the language, this would suggest that the change from a proper adjective to a verb is the result of an intermediate step where the proper adjective first becomes a noun, then a verb. This will be examined in greater depth in Section 4.3 in the discussion of patterning in brand name change.

Noun-Adjective (Attributive)

A further type of change, and one that is very productive both in generic brand names and in other common nouns, is the change from a noun to an attributive adjective. Once ellipsis occurs, rendering the proper adjective a proper, then common noun, the brand can be used generically as an attributive adjective modifying any common noun for which that name might appear accurate to the speaker. To offer an example of this, *Mace self-defense spray* reduces to *mace* after ellipsis, then can be attached to another noun; for our purposes, let's say, the common noun *canister*. The result is a fully acceptable noun phrase as in the sentence *She grabbed the mace canister from the glove compartment, spraying it in the general direction of Dan.*

Proper Adjective --> Adjective (Attributive)

This type of change occurs in only a few cases. *Day-Glo* to *day-glo(w)*, as in the sentence *The cheerleader had day-glow laces in her shoes*, exemplifies this type of change. What makes this type of change different from that noted above is that there is no corresponding noun form. It other words, *day-glow* has no noun. It would appear then that the change would be directly from proper noun to common adjective. Again, for this type of change to occur there must be no association to the brand in the mind of the speaker. The form is simply taken as an adjective, most likely learned without the association to the brand, in this case as 'fluorescent'.

In the next section I will look briefly at semantic broadening in brand names.

4.1.2 Semantic Changes: Broadening in Brand Names

While the grammatical changes in brand names are important to understanding how genericization works, it is the semantic broadening that occurs in these names which appears to set the grammatical changes in motion. It is only when the brand is perceived in the mind of the speaker to be a class term for a group of similar items, as opposed to a single specific entity, that the grammatical changes beyond ellipsis will occur. Whether mistakenly so, or as a conscious action, the addition of the class sense of the word is the essence of brand name change. To reiterate, semantic broadening refers to the extension of meaning. This, of course, can be accomplished in a number of ways. First, the simple extension of meaning most often found in generic changes of the sort I am interested in here is the extension from specific to generic. Put another way, the extension is from a single item of a particular company to the similar products produced by different companies. These changes I will refer to as Type-1 changes. Yet, it is worth noting that other types of semantic broadening do exist.

A second type of generic change is found in the new meanings arising that have little to do with the original brand. These cross-class changes are certainly far less frequent than Type-1 changes. One notable example is the brand name, *Oreo* (cookies). A case can certainly be made for *Oreo* as having undergone a Type-1 generic change, applicable to any similar chocolate sandwich cookie with vanilla cream filling. But, at the same time a separate meaning has developed apart from that of the cookie. In particular, *Oreo* has come to be the term (often derogatory) for an African-American who acts too much like a Caucasian. Another example is the common use of *spam* to refer to junk e-mail. While this type of change (I will call these Type-2 changes) is not the focus of this study, these changes remain an area for further study in the future.

4.2 A Proposed Pattern of Brand Name Change

Having briefly touched upon the types of grammatical changes involved in genericization and the role semantic broadening plays in these changes, I can now turn to what is likely to be a hierarchy of generic brand name change. The hierarchy that I will suggest at this point is tentative, one that will be borne out in the data of the following two chapters. The underlying assumption however, is that there is a pattern. For there not to be a regular pattern, the changes we see in brand names would have to be far more random than they are, and the creation of a corpus would likely have been far more difficult. Yet, virtually nothing in the Type-1 changes appears unique; the assumption therefore is that a regular patterned process governs genericization. The proposed pattern is exhibited in the figure that follows.

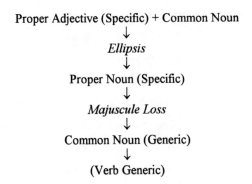

**Figure 1. Hierarchy of Grammatical and Semantic Change in
Brand Names (Excluding Adjectives)**

In the first figure, the hierarchy is quite straightforward. All brand names
begin legally as proper adjectives with a specific reference to the product or
products of a particular producer. These proper adjectives are followed by a
common generic (class) noun (e.g., *Xerox* photocopiers). In the first step, ellipsis
of the common noun occurs, resulting in the realization of the proper adjective as
a proper noun. This is done rather naturally as very few speakers recognize that
brand names are proper adjectives. The general assumption is therefore that brand
names are proper nouns. McMahon's earlier remark (see Section 4.1.1) on
ellipsis as a two-part expression where the second becomes redundant and
ultimately drops accurately describes what happens in this step. We are then left
with a proper noun with specific reference, that of the brand name as the name for
the product itself (as opposed to simply the maker of the product).

The next step is the shift from specific reference to that product alone to
generic reference for the class of items. When the association to the class occurs,
the name is no longer fully recognized as the brand name. It may entirely remain
applicable to the brand itself in the minds of many speakers, but will also be
useful as the name for other similar products. Frequently, it is the loss of the

majuscule in writing that signals both that the brand has added a generic sense, and secondly, that the brand name has also become a generic common noun. It is important to stress here that the name may remain in the minds of many a brand name, capitalized, and specific. As with any change in progress, there will be both conservative and innovative speakers of the language. At this point we can refer back to Grace's (1997, 1997b) discussion of the speakers' knowledge of language. As speakers of the language, our KOL, according to Grace, is slightly modified through each contact with other speakers. It would then not be uncommon for us to learn new brand names as we would any new word, possibly as a brand, or simply as a class-noun.

Many brand names stop at the stage of becoming a common generic noun, being utilized both as a specific and a generic referent. Some brand names of this sort immediately come to mind are *Coke* and *coke*, as everyone recognizes it as a brand name, but many people may ask for *a coke* and are served *Pepsi* or *RC*.[21] In many cases it is a cola-flavored beverage they want, not a particular company's product, whether a product of *Coca-Cola* or a product produced by anyone else. Pharmaceutical products of the same ingredients, or for the same benefit, frequently do this. *Tylenol* and *a tylenol*, *Tampax* and *a tampax*, and others typify this. In other cases however, the association to the brand may be lost or nearly lost altogether as the change runs its course. By the time the change is completed it is only the legal proprietary status that holds on to the specific reference. Many brand names have approached this disassociation of the name to a specific company's product. Some examples of this are *band aids*, *mace*, *ping pong*, *astroturf*, *crock pot*, *frisbee*, and *windbreaker*. All of these remain brand names legally, but they no longer have any association to a brand in the minds of many consumers. Once the change is completed however, the legal protection may then

---

[21] Coca-Cola has attacked this practice vigorously. Where it was once common to ask for *a coke* and to be served any cola-based drink, a common practice now has become a follow-up question by the server if the cola beverage of the establishment is *Pepsi* or *RC*. This does not, however, preclude the speaker from requesting a coke generically.

be stripped. This is of course what has happened to many former brand names such as *cellophane, aspirin, thermos,* and *cube steak.* If we consider the above examples, we can see this type of change as a continuum, where many changes are fully generic (that is no longer recognized by anyone as generic and subsequently having lost protection), and others are in various stages of genericization.

While for many brand names becoming a common noun is the final step, some others take the process of change one step further with the adding of a generic action verb. *To xerox* (<a xerox), *to mace someone* (<mace), and *to rollerblade* (<rollerblades) demonstrate this point. It appears likely also that this and the other changes above are ordered changes. I have found no cases for example, of a generic verb without there also being a corresponding generic noun. This will be examined further in the analysis of the data.

Figure 1 demonstrated the generic shift to a noun or verb, but this figure excluded the change from a proper adjective to a common adjective. As a change, this is a rather rare occurrence (as in the *day-glow* example). It also fails to appear with a noun variant. This in turn suggests a separate change. The resulting pattern for this type of change appears below.

Proper Adjective (Specific) + Common Noun
↓
Common Attributive Adjective (Generic)

Figure 2. Pattern of Generic Change to an Adjective

In the type of change exemplified in Figure 2, only a single change appears to be involved. This change is from a proper adjective with specific reference to a common adjective with generic reference. The association is not to a particular product however. Rather, as adjectives serve a descriptive function, the association is to anything exhibiting the property or quality exemplified by the now-common adjective. Our example of *Day-Glo* above matches this change pattern. The *Day-Glo* name, as a brand name applied to a series of products and colors all exemplifying the shared quality of bright fluorescence, has resulted in the common adjective possessing the generic sense of fluorescent. Again the loss of the majuscule is one of the triggering factors in this change, the result being *day-glo*, *day-glow*, or *day glow*. As noted above, this type of change is far less common than the other types. Once the common noun is dropped genericization has occurred. The resulting common adjective can then attach to any noun bearing that quality, regardless of semantic class. This last qualifier is quite important because it demonstrates a primary difference between the changes of Figure 1 and of those in Figure 2. The changes in Figure 1 all become generic for items in the same semantic class. The resulting adjectives however, can be applied to any item so long as it is perceived to bear a similar quality to that of the adjective. A second important point differentiating Figures 1 and 2 is that while we can see both the proper adjective and adjective variants, we do not however see a noun (i.e., a day-glo(w)). It does seem entirely plausible though, as does the potential verb *to day-glo(w) something* with a meaning 'to make fluorescent'.

In the next section I will present in greater detail my hypotheses of how genericization works and the factors contributing to these changes. The hypotheses are based upon the belief that there are contributing factors which create an environment for genericization to occur. The formal presentation of the hypotheses of this theory and subsequent discussion will lead to the actual experiments involved in testing the theory in Chapter 5.

4.3 Hypotheses

The hypotheses that make up the theory of genericization were constructed during four years of examination of brand names in English. Those hypotheses appearing below focus upon what appear to be the contributing factors which will instigate generic brand-name change. An explanation of the testing of these hypotheses will follow this description.

> H1. If A is a brand name for an innovative product (one which did not exist before), then the association of that item with its name will become synonymous, rendering the brand name both a product name, and the name for the entire class.

Hypothesis 1 considers the issue of innovation. Innovation in language creates novel forms. This fact is widely known. In terms of the creativity in product development, when a new product enters the market, if the product did not exist prior, the name may be taken not as the name of the maker of the product, but as the product itself. Furthermore, as the product did not exist prior, no class name will then exist. Frequently a company will propose a novel class name (for legal purposes), effectively creating a new semantic class, alongside the brand name of the innovative product. This however does little because it is the brand name that is given the exposure through advertising and not the novel class noun. The result then is that the new brand name will extend to the class name as well, a generic class name for all subsequent products in the newly-developed class. Hypothesis 1 can be restated in terms of the following formula.

product name	class name		product name	class name
A	$\varnothing$		A $\rightarrow$	A

Figure 3. Genericization as a Result of Innovation

To apply the hypothesis realized in Figure 3 we can utilize the brand name *Rollerblade*. When *Rollerblade* first appeared on the market the product was a significant upgrade from their predecessor *rollerskates*. They carried a single track and could be used more effectively outdoors than *rollerskates*. As a new product, no class term existed for this innovation. The company producing

Rollerblades tried, in vain, to introduce the expression *in-line skates*. However, by the time they had reached limited success with the created class name (it has taken some ten years now), the brand name had become both a noun and a verb. This can be again exhibited in the second formula.

product name class name   product name class name
Rollerblades   ∅   Rollerblades → rollerblades

Figure 4. Generic Change as a Result of Innovation

In Figure 4, I have called the rollerblade class name ∅. Despite there being a created class name, in essence the result is the same as not having any class name at all. To reiterate a point made above, the advertising goes into the brand and not into the class-noun. Therefore, it can be considered to be a functional zero.

Other examples I would consider to have changed to generic brand names on the basis of hypothesis one are *mace, xerox,* and *thermos.*

H2. If the predominant brand name in a semantic class (e.g., types of over-the-counter pain killers) is shorter than the corresponding class-noun, that predominant brand name will become the generic for the entire semantic class.

Hypothesis 2 is based on what has been called the law of least effort, or Zipf's law (Zipf 1935). In many parts of the language we can see the preference for simplicity. Acronyms, clippings, abbreviations, contractions, and ellipsis all suggest that in many cases speakers are trying to eliminate much of the redundancy found throughout language. Applying the law of least effort to brand names, the market leader in a particular category that bears a name that is shorter than the class name is a likely candidate to succumb to genericization. This hypothesis can be demonstrated in Figure 5 below.

81

product name class name   product name   class name
    a1   bb   a1   →   a1

Figure 5. Genericization by Simplicity

In Figure 5, a brand name noted as a in primary market position (1) that is shorter in terms of syllable length than the class term (bb) will then provide an environment for genericization to occur. This hypothesis is illustrated in the example below.

product name class name   product name class name
   Jell-O   gelatin   Jell-O   →   jello

Figure 6. Genericization by Simplicity

In this example, the brand name Jell-O is a two syllable brand name, while the class name gelatin is three syllables. The result is a generic brand name, *jello*. Other examples of brand names in this category are *xerox* (cf. photocopier, photocopy), *pop tart* (cf. toaster pastry), and *Q-tip* (cf. cotton swab). In the presentation and analysis of the corpus, the rapidity with which this type of change may occur will become evident. This is primarily due to the verbose noun phrases used in lieu of a simple common noun. The common noun phrase for the brand name *Velcro* is the daunting *hook and loop fastener*.

H3. Ellipsis of the common noun is a prerequisite for generic brand-name change. The process is ellipsis of the common noun which in turn results in a grammatic shift from proper adjective to proper noun. The next step is proper noun to common noun. The common noun then may become a verb.

82

Hypotheses 3 has been discussed in section 4.2, and will not be restated here.

> H4. There must be a psychological association between a brand name and a single product. It appears that brand names which represent items from a number of different classes are much more difficult to attach a generic meaning to. For example, the brand name *Tylenol* can be attached to any over-the-counter pain reliever (excluding aspirin), and is only associated with that purpose. Compare that to *Chanel* which makes a multitude of different products (perfume, clothing, etc.). In other words, a generic meaning cannot be assigned because there is no single item association to be made.

Hypothesis 4 is what I will refer to as the *Single-Association Hypothesis*. The Single-Association Hypothesis distinguishes brand names of a single product class, as different from those that name a multitude of different products. In cursory observation of a sample of generic brand names, it became apparent that there was a relationship between those product names that represented a single product, and those that were used to represent a number of products. Those names that were used for a number of diverse products appear to be much less likely to become generic brand names. Those however with a single product association had the ability to become a generic name. Further examination will be undertaken to try to disprove each of these hypotheses.

A final point regarding these hypotheses is that they are not mutually exclusive. A generic brand name may have one or more of these characteristics. Similarly, a brand name may share one or more of these characteristics and not become generic.

4.4 Corpus Construction and Procedure

4.4.1 Creation of the Corpus

The design of a corpus against which the theory of genericization could be tested was challenging. The identification of a number of brand names believed to be generic was in itself quite simple however. To this end, I began by identifying 100 brand names I believed to be generic brand names from the roughly 4,000 trade and service marks of the International Trademark Association's 1994 *Trademark Checklist*. These were then compiled into a table. Each of the brand names included was then followed by the prescribed generic noun or noun phrase. However, at this point, and feeling that an introspective selection of generic brands may be perceived in a similar way to stacking the deck in poker, I chose to abandon the first corpus table. This would be the first of three compilations done to secure a 100-name corpus, the third compilation of which appears in Appendix A. In place of the first corpus, I chose to refer back to a series of articles on generic brand names including Adams 1987, Hughes 1988, Lederer 1985, and Lentine and Shuy 1990.[22] In addition to the brand names extracted from the articles above, brand names included in the trademark education ads of *Writer's Digest* were also entered into the corpus. The trademark education ads are constructed as a means of 'educating' the public against misuse. As noted in Chapter 1, it is because the name is being, to use the company's words, 'misused', that they are advertising against these uses. If one takes this to be the case, then the brands advertised in these ads can then be seen to be generic. In the articles and *Writer's Digest* advertisements it was possible to identify 90 brand names that had been referred to by the authors as generic. To these, I added an additional 10 to create a corpus of 100. The number 100 is not entirely arbitrary. Rather, it provides a round number that is both easy for calculations

---

[22] One book also contributed brand names to the corpus (Landau 1994).

and easy to read for the readers of this work who will be interested in forming their own judgments about the results.

Once this second compilation of 100 brand names was completed, the corpus was then listed alphabetically in a table consisting of five columns. The first column contains the generic form or forms of the brand name. The generic form of the brand name was determined in a number of ways. First, if the generic term only carries a single spelling pattern with no variants then it was listed as such (e.g., coke, mace). In cases where variant spellings in the generic were possible (day glow, day-glow, day-glo) the variations were listed.

The second column of the corpus contained the brand name followed by its common class-noun or noun phrase (in italics) as listed in the Trademark Checklist. On some occasions, the generic brand name was not one of the 4,000 brands on the list. In these cases, a check of the company's web site (where available), or in some cases a telephone call to the INTA, provided the necessary information.

The third column of the corpus table includes the name of the company that produces the product. As noted earlier, the brand name and the trade name (company name) may be the same. This information may be important in ascertaining what percentage of names actually follows this pattern. As will be seen in the upcoming chapter on cross-linguistic notions of genericization, in Japanese it is frequently the company name and not the brand name that is important, being seen as a way of establishing cross-product brand loyalty.

The fourth column consists of the grammatical category or categories of the generic brand. In some cases, this was easily identifiable on the basis of examples in the sample articles. In others, the *Oxford English Dictionary* was employed. The identification of the grammatical category of the brand was the final step in the construction of the corpus. The importance of this step as the final one was again to again insure that the analysis was separate from the construction of the corpus.

The final column of the table was reserved for the source of the generic brand name. As noted, 90 of the 100 brand names were selected on the basis of inclusion in a number of articles on the subject of generic brand names. For each of these 90 brand names, the source mentioning that name was entered into this column. The remaining ten were left blank. This disclosure of the source makes for a clearer understanding of the construction of the corpus.

At the point where examples were sought to verify brand names entered into the second corpus, further revisions were made. This is discussed in greater detail in Section 5.1.

4.4.2 Challenging the Corpus

The series of articles from which the corpus was constructed provided little methodology for ascertaining the status of a brand name. Only the article by Lentine and Shuy took a pragmatic approach to identifying tokens of the brand name with an extended semantic range. The others identified generic brand names, but failed to mention precisely how the determination of genericization was made. Concerned with this flaw in the data collection, I chose to follow a similar strategy to that employed by Lentine and Shuy. In their study of the prefix *Mc-*, Lentine and Shuy employed the Nexis national clipping service of newspaper and magazine articles over a two-month period. The system works as a concordancer, identifying key word tokens from the various print media. While technical constraints within the university where the original research was conducted,[23] and the cost constraints of private registration, prohibited the use of the Nexis database employed by Lentine and Shuy, an alternative system was employed. To begin, I approached the *OED*. The *OED* provides examples in each sense and in novel usage. For this research however, and in contrast to the

---

[23] The only access to Nexis at the University of Hawaii is through the law library. The library restricts access to the database to the members of the law school only.

classification of tokens utilized by Lentine and Shuy, two documented uses from different sources beyond that of a brand name with specific reference to a particular company were considered grounds for inclusion as a generic brand name. Tokens were selected on the basis of a number of criteria. First, all of the tokens extracted to establish genericization are from written English, and within the written medium the loss of capitalization strongly suggests that the brand name is no longer recognized as anything other than a common noun. Similarly, in a number of cases, the brand name in lowercase would appear next to another brand name that was capitalized. This too would suggest that the brand name in lowercase was indeed generic. An example of this use of brand names is found in the following token, *The silicone gel is cut slightly larger than the wound and covered with a Band-Aid, ace bandage, cloth wrap or tape.* In this example *Ace bandage*, a brand name, is in lowercase, whereas *Band-Aid*, another brand name, remains capitalized. A second example is found in this sentence, *Here's a list of things we are ALWAYS in need of: ..dry cat chow, paper towels, Kleenex ...* In this example the brand name being used as a generic is *Cat Chow* (cf. Kleenex). In other cases, semantic information provided evidence for generic use of the brand. In some cases, an uppercase token was selected when it was evident that the usage remained generic *You'll hear this kind of pool called a 'Jacuzzi', because the Jacuzzi firm pioneered in this application of the hydro-jet.* This example leaves the offset form *Jacuzzi* capitalized, but the meaning of the sentence is that all pools of this kind are called a Jacuzzi because the original version of this pool was produced by the Jacuzzi company. An additional example is as follows: *Some people use the term Wiffle Ball for any plastic ball.* Again the brand is capitalized, but the meaning of the sentence demonstrates the generic meaning. In cases where the *OED* did not list a given brand, these brands were set aside for further examination in a second manner. There are a number of reasons why a brand may not have been included in the *OED*. First, the *OED*, while attempting to be comprehensive, is always behind the language by a number of years. The last *OED* was published in 1989 and while biannual supplements appear frequently, many names are not included. Moreover, the OED is a product of British scholarship, which may simply have less exposure to the many domestic products present 'stateside'. To offer some balance to this, and to increase the corpus to a desired 100 brands, the Internet was then employed for the remaining tokens. The World Wide Web provided an array of natural tokens, many of which came from discussion groups and personal home pages. As these are generally unedited, the language is unhindered to a great extent from the ploys to invoke proprietary right and 'proper usage' upon the brand.[24]

Finally, it is worth noting the rationale for selecting more than one token for each brand as evidence of genericization. Two tokens were selected as a means of avoiding the fluke occurrence of a single token, either by a typographical error, or by pure coincidence. By requiring two uses from different sources, it is believed that this will insure a level of accuracy beyond introspection for showing why a given brand name was included. These tokens and the sample sentences in which they occur are included in Appendix B.

4.4.3 Testing the Hypotheses

A selection of tests was devised to challenge each hypothesis. Each of these and their tests will be examined individually. The actual discussion of the results of the tests, however, will be reserved for the next chapter.

> H1. If A is a brand name for an innovative product (one which did not exist before), then the association of that item with its name will become synonymous, rendering the brand name both a product name, and the name for the entire class.

---

[24] While this is indeed the case, on more than one occasion I entered web sites which noted that they had been reprimanded for misusing the brand name. The advantage however is that clipping services and the brand holders themselves simply cannot keep up with the number of new web sites and personal home pages coming on line.

88

This hypothesis focuses on innovation, not only of the brand name but of the class name as well. When a new product enters the market for which no other similar product previously existed, then the company introducing that product will attempt to introduce a common class-noun or noun phrase as well. Still, the problem with this effort is that the advertising budget of the company goes toward marketing the brand name and not the class name. In effect, the users of the language have little choice other than to use the brand name, when that is what is presented to them. In order to test Hypothesis 1, a single test will be employed. A simple examination of the 100 generic brand names will be undertaken. Those names for products which are the sole product in their category, or which may no longer be the sole product but which may be seen as the original producer of the product, will be tabulated.

> H2. If the predominant brand name in a semantic class(e.g., types of over-the-counter pain killers) is shorter than the corresponding class-noun, that predominant brand name will become the generic for the entire semantic class.

Hypothesis 2 refers back to the law of least effort. As with the first hypothesis, the testing of Hypothesis 2 involves a corpus-based tabulation of those brand names which are shorter than the generic common noun, in terms of the number of syllables, the number of words, and the mean length of utterance. It is expected that a significant percentage of the corpus will be brand names shorter than the class-noun.

> H3. Ellipsis of the common noun is a prerequisite for generic brand-name change. The process is ellipsis of the common noun which in turn results in a grammatic shift from proper adjective to proper noun. The next step is proper noun to common noun. The common noun then may become a verb, etc.

The third hypothesis is based upon the theory that generic brand-name change is patterned. I have proposed two separate patterns, one for nouns and verbs, and the other for adjectives. To test this hypothesis, the grammatical categories for each brand name have been listed in the corpus. If the pattern is correct, the evidence will then support a hierarchical process. In other words, if there is a generic verb then there will also be either a generic noun or generic adjective. For this test, the percentage of tokens in each grammatical category will be tabulated. Then, those cases other than generic nouns will be examined to determine whether the suggested hierarchical pattern is valid. Any exceptions to the pattern will be discussed.

> H4. There must be a psychological association between a brand name and a single product. It appears that brand names which represent items from a number of different classes are much more difficult to attach a generic meaning to. For example, the brand name *Tylenol* can be attached to any over-the-counter pain reliever (excluding aspirin), and is only associated with that purpose. Compare that to *Chanel*, which makes a multitude of different products (perfume, clothing, etc.). In other words, a generic meaning cannot be assigned because there is no single item association to be made.

The testing of the fourth hypothesis will be done in two parts. First, based upon the corpus, those brand names listed with a single generic class name will be separated from those representing multiple products. The percentages then will be calculated and set into a table. What is expected is that very few generic brands will be applicable to multiple products of different classes. The results will then provide information as to whether there is a single-product association with generic brands.

4.4.4 Testing for Counterevidence

To this point, the treatment of the hypotheses, and the tests that are to be employed, has focused primarily upon trying to validate the hypotheses. However, it is equally important to consider how testing might disprove the hypotheses. In other words, what counterevidence would be necessary to nullify any or all of these hypotheses? It is best to return to the testing of each hypothesis.

Hypothesis 1 argues that novel forms create novel classes, increasing the likelihood for genericization to occur. To reiterate, the test of this hypothesis seeks out those brand names which represent(ed) novel classes (e.g., *Rollerblade*, *Hula Hoop*, etc.) For Hypothesis 1 to be falsified, a brand name for a new product of a novel semantic class with primary market share would not become generic.

Hypothesis 2 will be tested for length in terms of syllable, word, and mean length of utterance. This examination measures the average length of each brand name, and is tabulated and divided out by the total number of entries (here 100). The anticipation is that the mean length of each of these tests on the generic brand names will be shorter than those same tests run against the common class-nouns. As counterevidence to this hypothesis, the mean average for class-nouns in each of the three tests would have to be shorter, in terms of syllable, word, and mean length, than the corresponding generic brand names.

Hypothesis 3 centers on the principle that genericization is regular. The process is set forth in Figures 1 and 2. The testing of Hypothesis 3 involves an examination of the grammatical forms present for each generic brand name (see Column 4 of Appendix A). There are at least two ways Hypothesis 3 could be rendered invalid. First, we would need to find counterexamples to the processes presented in Figures 1 and 2. For example, do we find a generic verb form but not a generic noun? Are there generic adjectives, but no corresponding generic nouns? Then, we would need to find a random distribution in the generic changes in brand names. In other words, we would need to find no sustainable patterns, or counterexamples we cannot account for with our process of genericization.

Finally, Hypothesis 4, the Single-Association Hypothesis, states that only brand names with an association to a single product can become generic. The test for Hypothesis 4 examines the association(s) of each brand name. For Hypothesis 4 to be voided, a brand name with multiple associations to products of differing semantic classes would have to become generic.

The analysis to follow will shed light upon these possible counterexamples. However, we will operate under the assumption that these hypotheses are valid until such point where we can find sufficient counterevidence against them.

In Chapter 5, statistical information regarding the brand names included within the corpus, and the tests mentioned in section 4.4.3 above to test Hypotheses 1-4 will be applied and the results presented for analysis in Chapter 6.

CHAPTER V. APPLICATION OF THE THEORY OF GENERICIZATION

"What sort of insects do you rejoice in, where you come from?" the
Gnat inquired.
"I don't rejoice in insects at all", Alice explained, "because I'm
rather afraid of them - at least the large kinds. But I can tell you
the names of some of them."
"Of course they answer to their names?" the Gnat remarked carelessly.
"I never knew them to do it."
"What's the use of their having names", the Gnat said, "if they won't
answer to them?"
"No use to them," said Alice, "but it's useful to the people that name them,
I suppose. If not, why do things have names at all?"
"I can't say," the Gnat replied.
                    -Lewis Carroll, (1872) Through the Looking-Glass

In this chapter, each of the four hypotheses will be tried against the tests
mentioned in Chapter 4. However, it is important first to look briefly at the
demographic information inherent in the 100 names in the corpus. This chapter
will therefore consist of five sections, with the first section focusing on
background and each of the remaining four sections focusing on the testing of a
single hypothesis. Upon completion of each test, the results will be presented.
Analysis of the results, however, will be reserved for Chapter 6.

5.1 Statistical Background Information

As noted in Chapter 4, the second selection of generic brand names to be included in the corpus was made on the basis of a selection of articles touching on the subject of generic brand names. Those articles produced 41 brand names in the final corpus and these are marked as such in Appendix A. It should be reiterated here that regardless of the source of the generic brand name, inclusion in the final corpus was based upon two verifiable tokens of generic use from the *OED* or Internet. This accounts for the differences attested in the corpus between the first and second attempts at creating a corpus (see Section 4.4.1) and the final corpus actually used in testing. Added to these 41 were brand names promoting trademark education as found in writing craft magazines such as *Writer's Digest.* These advertisements contributed an additional 20 generic brand names. Finally, I added the remaining 39 names as a result of three factors: First, brand names were added on the basis of token sentences used to establish genericization in the above 61 brand names where more than one generic brand in the same sentence was exhibited. In other words, serial listings of generic brand names in the token sentences provided additional corpus entries. Additionally, suggestions made by classmates and colleagues familiar with my work were considered and once genericization was formally established these too were added to the corpus. Finally, I added the remaining brand names to the corpus on the basis of introspection and personal preference, drawing on material found on the Internet. In some cases, brand names believed to be generic, including those in articles, ads, and those I believed to be generic could not be proven generic on the basis of the criteria of two tokens from different sources. In other words, for many brands I could not identify two generic tokens in writing (excluding my ability to construct an acceptable and grammatical generic sentence). Some of these included *Cheerios* (Writer's Digest ad), *Cuisinart* (Lentine/Shuy) and *Raid* (my choice). This then accounts for the difference seen here and in the construction of the corpus as presented in Chapter 4 (where I stated 90 names were from the articles and Writer's Digest). In many of the names in the original corpus, genericization was not established. This is not to say however that these brand names are not, or could not be generic. It simply acknowledges the constraint of how long one desires to look to find acceptable examples of a brand name in generic use.

Of the 100 brand names in the final corpus, the tokens used to demonstrate generic use were attained from both the *Oxford English Dictionary* and the Internet. In particular, 55 of the brand names in the final corpus were listed in the *OED*, and of these 55, 45 provided the necessary two generic examples. The remaining 10 were listed in the *OED*, and of those, 5 provided one example, and 5 were listed but provided no examples in generic use. Therefore to complete the corpus, tokens for the 5 brand names needing a single token and for the remaining 50 brand names were taken solely from the Internet. The 45 OED names, 50 Internet names, and 5 mixed names then account for the entire 100 name corpus. The entire list with the tokens for each and a selection of relevant information is included in Appendix B.

Upon completion of the researching and charting of the 100 brand names a discovery was made that 5 of the brand names in the corpus were no longer legally recognized as brand names. These names have undergone the full change of genericization, and are no longer recognized legally as brands. These 5 are *hovercraft, thermos, TV dinner, technicolor,* and *teleprompter*. The 5 will remain in the corpus however and will be treated the same as the remaining 95 names. This can be done because, although these names are no longer brands recognized by the law, they are still brand names historically, and a very strong argument can be made that there is no difference between a *TV dinner* (with no legal protection) and a *yo-yo* (a registered brand name, but one which is recognized by virtually no one). Language has no concern for legal recognition.

5.1.1 Morphosyntactic Corpus Data

In searching for the triggers of generic brand-name change it is important to examine all of the possible contributing factors to this type of change. Following the list of morphosyntactic changes in McMahon 1994:193ff a number of important points regarding the corpus can be made. It should be noted from the onset however, that overlap in some cases does occur, with some brand names exhibiting more than a single type of strategy. To begin, when the 100 generic brand names were listed, 10 of the brand names could not be written in the generic form without the inclusion of the common class-noun. The common noun then becomes part of a compound noun. Examples of this include *ace bandage*, *allen wrench*, *brillo pad* and so forth. From these examples we can see that names such as *Ace* have meanings beyond the brand. Asking for *an Ace* in the context of requesting a bandage will get one nowhere, the name then cannot compete against the more common contextualization of an Ace in poker (or any of its other uses). This should not be misconstrued as violating Hypothesis 4 (the Single-Association Hypothesis). Once the name is used with the common noun and the compounding has taken place, the association becomes a single association. The point here is that in order to distinguish the name from its other possible uses the name is attached to the generic class-noun, the entire compound becoming a generic name.

In the corpus it was quite difficult to assess the word length, as many of these brand names were actually combinations or even larger phrases.[25] Combinations include three different forms. The first form of combination is found when we have two separate lexemes rising as a single unit but for which the boundary remains. This type of combination forms with brand names such as *allen wrench* which is made up of both the brand, here *Allen*, and the class-noun

---

[25] While the focus of this study was textual data, a better test for the treatment of these combinations would be to elicit the forms in speaking in order to examine the placement of the stress (e.g., white house vs. White House).

wrench, which has become a single lexical unit. In the corpus, more than a quarter of the corpus (26) were combinations. Examples such as *Cat Chow, Hula Hoop*, and *Magic Marker* demonstrate this point. Of these 26, 10 were of the type mentioned in the previous paragraph, those requiring the common noun in the generic name.

The second type of combination includes those brand names that are hyphenated. The use of the hyphen of course is a grammatical function that suggests that the relationship between the two lexical items more closely resembles a single lexical item than two separate units. As the *OED* (1989: xxxi) notes the hyphen 'implies .. that the syntactic relation between two words is closer than if they stood side by side without it ..' Where the two words with no boundary can be seen as a true compound, the hyphenation can be seen to be one step off from full compounding. In the corpus this was found to be a productive way of forming brand names, with 17 names employing this strategy. *Band-Aid, Ben-Gay*, and *Crock-Pot* are examples of this process. In these examples, in addition to the hyphenation, we can also see the use of capitalization of both words.

The third type of combination, the traditional compound, is made up of two lexemes that have combined to form a single lexical item, and for which the boundary has been lost. In the corpus this type of combination was found in eight brands. *Hovercraft, Windbreaker, Rollerblade* typify this compounding.

Similar to compounding is affixation and this too is present in the corpus. In the corpus it was possible to identify 11 brand names possessing an affix, with 4 utilizing prefixes and 7 with suffixes. The most prevalent affix in the data, appearing in 5 names, was the *-o* suffix as found in *Bondo, Brasso, Drano, Exacto (knife)* and *Jell-O*.[26]

---

[26] The meaning of the *-o* suffix is unclear. What is known however, is that the *-o* suffix was popular for naming food products at the beginning of this century.

98

Clipping was evident in two brand names in the corpus, *Gore-Tex* (<Gore Textiles) and *Pine Sol* (<Pine Solvent).

Blending was a frequent process in the corpus. It is possible here to separate blends into three groups. The first group is made up of blends in the traditional sense, namely those which would normally turn up in language. In the case of brand names however, these are often graphologically unusual. *ReaLemon* (<real+lemon) and *SweeTarts* (<sweet+tarts), the only two forms of this type in the corpus, typify this point with the blend being made with the elimination of one or the other of the duplicated consonants, either the final consonant of the first word or the initial consonant of the second. Note the majusculization of the remaining blended consonant in the middle of the new lexical item/compound.[27] The second type of blend is similar to the first and takes a part of one form and combines it with a part of another form to create a new word. Often this involves the front part of one word, and the back part of another word to form a novel form. This occurred in three forms, *Spam* (<spiced ham), *Muzak* (<music+Kodak), and *Rolodex* (<rolling+index). In one case, *Velcro* the blend was made between the front portions of two words (<velours croch). In other cases, the attachment of part of one form was to an entirely different word where the second form remains unchanged. This is found in three cases: *Dictaphone* (<dictate+phone), *Tampax* (<tampon+packs), *Technicolor* (<technical+color). Finally, the third type of blend is particularly unusual as it involves the extraction of parts of a word or words to form a new form, often from the middle of the forms. Four names exhibited this pattern: *Dramamine* (<diphenhydra<+ma>mine), *Novocain* (<Lat. novus+<+o>cocaine), *Styrofoam* (>polystyrene+<+o>+foam), and *Teflon* (<polytetrafluoroethylene).

---

[27] It is important to note here that while there is orthographic degemination, phonetically these forms are still pronounced as geminates.

5.1.2 Additional Considerations

Having now looked at a number of different considerations, we can now look at syllable length, an area believed to be quite important to the occurrence of genericization. Rather than taking each word separately, syllable length per brand will be measured by taking the brand name as a whole unit. It is important to do this because when we replace a common noun with the generic brand that brand is replaceable as a unit. For the purposes of this study, where the unit is a combination, the number of syllables will be the number of syllables of the entire combination, as if it were a true compound. In the corpus, the average name length of generic brand names was 2.57 syllables. More specifically, 5 brand names were single-syllable names. In addition, there were 44 two-syllable names, 41 three-syllable names, 9 four-syllable names, and 1 five-syllable name. There were no brand names in the corpus longer than five syllables.

In Section 3.3.1 it was noted that trademark law identifies four types of brand name; fanciful or coined names, arbitrary names, suggestive marks, and descriptive marks. To reiterate, fanciful names are those such as Kodak that are made-up and which have no inherent meaning in them. In contrast, arbitrary names are those which are existing English words but which bear no relationship to the product bearing the name. *Apple* for computers is typical of this type of name. Suggestive names are those which highlight a perceived quality or benefit of the product. *Coppertone* for tanning oil is a good representative of this type of name. The final type of brand, and the one offered the least protection under the law, is the descriptive brand. These brands describe the goods and services rather than simply naming them. *Homemakers* for housekeeping services shows this process. In light of these four types of brand names, an examination of the corpus was made to see whether a pattern in generic brand names developed. In the corpus of 100 names the following was found. There were 15 names identified into the coined marks list. 21 names were found to be arbitrary marks.

27 brand names carried at least one attribute of the product in the name and therefore were considered suggestive marks. Finally, 37 names were noted as descriptive trademarks. It is important to note how I approached this classification with the data. Names which etymologically were invented names and those names which were created by extracting parts of for example a scientific name (e.g., *Dramamine<di*phenhyd*ramine*) to create a previously non-existent name were put into class one. It can be said that as these scientific names are not normally in the public domain that the invented names bear no meaning to the speakers, thus they can be classified in the first class. Arbitrary marks, or those words existing in the language, but which are applied to products with no connection to the name include common nouns applied this way (e.g., *Scotch* for tape), but also family names applied to a product (e.g., *Allen* wrench). Suggestive names and descriptive names were separated on the basis of whether the name was perceived to be a quality of the product or the product itself. This difference can be seen for example in the difference between *Frigidaire* (class 3) and *Fiberglas* (class 4). *Frigidaire* was deliberately designed to literally refer to the cold air provided by the refrigerator while *Fiberglas* describes quite well the product itself.

If we now consider similarities in the brand names of the corpus a number of notable points surface. First, the largest group of generic brand names in the corpus is those having to do with food and drink, as well as the implements utilized for the preparation and preservation of food. Of the 100 brand names in the corpus, 29 were of this category. This was the category bearing by far the most generic brand names. The second most prevalent category was made of up items that can be said to be found in a bathroom. These included medicines, household cleaners, and toiletries. 16 brand names were found to be of this category. The remaining classifications are as follows: school/office supplies and related (14), hardware items (13), clothing items and materials (8), electronics and peripheral information (6), toys (5), pet supplies (4), vehicles (2), law enforcement supplies (2), places (1).

I now turn to the ten construction strategies set out by Charmasson (using an existing item, composition, fusion, derivation, clipping, misspellings, analogy, ideophones, and multimedia names) for brand names found in 3.3.2, a run of the corpus was conducted to attempt to classify the 100 names according to these strategies. This was no easy task and many of the names employed more than a single strategy. It became clear early in the run that an additional category would be required to account for the completely new Kodak-type names, as I was unable to find a way of classifying these names in Charmasson's 1988 classification. As such, an additional category was considered to account for these names. The findings in this classification are as follows. There were 21 arbitrary names (as noted in the classification based upon 3.3.1). Composition was the most prevalent category, one which comprised 41 brand names. The third category, fusion, resulted in only 2 names, while derivation was slightly more productive with 8 names. 15 names were developed as a result of clipping, and 17 names employed orthographic strategies, the so-called 'purposeful misspellings' and the addition of extra letters. Brand names developed on the basis of analogy comprised 7 places. The identification of ideophones was handled in a different manner and will be addressed in a moment. In 17 cases, it was believed that more than one strategy was in practice. In the final category, 2 names were found to be completely novel names.[28]

Returning now to the subject of the ideophones, it was exceptionally difficult to identify tokens in the initial run of the corpus. The exception to this is *Ping-Pong* which is likely to be an onomatopoeia mimicking the game. However, as many names in the corpus are simply combined forms of existing lexemes or arbitrary names based on existing forms, these can be excluded from consideration. In essence, only a select number of words from categories 4 (derivation), 6 (orthographic alterations + extra letters), 7 (analogy), and 11 (new

---

[28] A meticulous reader counting these totals will find that the total exceeds 100. the brand names were counted for each of the given strategies. Therefore, many of the names appear in the counts for more than a single strategy.

names) could be considered. This reduces the corpus to roughly a third. In many cases however, these names were also based upon existing forms and thus they eliminate themselves, except by coincidence, from consideration. Finally, this leaves us with a handful of names from the above groups and the two new names, *lycra* and *dacron*. Rather than examining a limited number of forms for what may be a limited number of tokens, and whereas the categorization of this strategy is not essential to this work, an examination of this category will be set aside. It therefore remains an additional area for further study.

One final tabulation that needs to be made is an examination of those brand names that are also company names, the dual function brand names. In examining the corpus, 20 of the brand names in the corpus were found to also be the name of the company.

This long introduction has sought to establish a basic understanding of the corpus, its construction, and the classification of the brands in the corpus on the basis of how they were constructed and on several criteria that will be important to the analysis in the next chapter. Now, it is time to turn to the testing of each of the four hypotheses on which the theory of genericization is based.

5.2 H1 (Innovation)

> H1. If A is a brand name for an innovative product (one which did not exist before), then the association of that item with its name will become synonymous, rendering the brand name both a product name, and the name for the entire class.

The testing of Hypothesis 1 involves a two-part examination of the corpus. First, brand names which are known to be the initial product in a class were selected. These, for example, include *slinky* and *rollerblade*. Once the first search was completed, then a second search, this time a search of the generic nouns and noun phrases, was undertaken. The purpose of this search is particularly to identify the names which employ longer phrases for generic nouns. It is likely that these would provide further evidence that when an innovative name came onto the market, no class name had existed and thus the rationale for the longer name. This can be demonstrated with the product *Velcro*. At the point where *Velcro* was developed no class name existed. No single word could be found to match the product and thus the phrase *hook and loop fasteners* was created. Some readers may believe that *Velcro fasteners* would have worked well. Yet, this is an incorrect assumption as fasteners of *Velcro* are only one (of many) kind of fasteners. In other words, *Velcro fasteners* is simply not distinct enough. This is an important point, and one that will be addressed in greater detail in Section 6.1. While not an entirely fool-proof identification method, the names believed to be innovative will be cross-checked against *OED* information (where available) and other sources such as Room 1982. Finally, a search of the Internet has turned up a number of short historical articles for companies which note the history of their particular brand.

If we now turn to the corpus, the first task was to identify the number of brand names which were innovative in their respective semantic classes. In the corpus, 50 brand names were found to be representative of novel or once-novel products. In some cases and classes, identification was quite easy. The five toys listed in the corpus were all innovative when first appearing on the market, and the result has been genericization. In others, it is quite clear that they are not the first company to produce the product. If we take *Ace* bandages for example, larger bandages have existed for centuries prior to the introduction of the *Ace bandage*. Ace simply added elastic to the product and, as a result, this example gained a prominent-enough status in the marketplace to become a generic brand name. In this case, it is not only Hypothesis 1 that is invoked, but also Hypothesis 2. This will be considered further when we get to the second hypothesis.

It was believed that by examining, in a second manner, the generic names attached to the brand name then this too might allude to innovation in the brand

104

name. However, this proved to be more difficult than was first thought. In some cases the longer generic names did develop as a result of innovation. However, in others they simply did not. To offer an example, the generic noun phrase for *Bake-Off* is 'cooking and baking contests', a wordy noun phrase, yet it would be irresponsible to say that Pillsbury invented the baking contest. Let us proceed to Hypothesis 2.

5.3 H2 (Length and Predominance)

> H2. If the predominant brand name in a semantic class (e.g., types of over-the-counter pain killers) is shorter than the corresponding class-noun, that predominant brand name will become the generic for the entire semantic class.

This hypothesis assumes that shorter brand names, and those which are easier to articulate, are more susceptible to genericization than are their longer and more complex counterparts. Predominance is also noted in this hypothesis, but can be equally applied to Hypothesis 1. If we simply look at the number of words alone, there is a clear difference. In the brand names the average name length was 1.4 words.[29] In direct contrast, in the generic nouns used to classify the brand, the average length was 2.1 words. It was noted earlier in section 5.1.1 that the average number of syllables per generic brand name was 2.6. Moreover, it was discovered that only 5 brand names were monosyllabic, 44 were disyllabic names, 41 trisyllabic names, 9 quatr-syllabic names, and 1 quin-syllabic name. No brand names were longer than five syllables. Applying the same collection strategy for the generic class-nouns and phrases that was employed for the generic brand

---

[29] For this count, hyphenated brands were treated individually. In cases where the hyphenated brand consisted of two separate and identifiable lexemes, they were treated as such. In cases where the hyphenated brand is treated as a single unit when generic, it was treated as a single lexical item for tabulation. Furthermore, in some cases generic brand names were noted with two or more variants. The first one was selected consistently in each of these cases.

names we can see how dramatic this hypothesis really is. Within the corpus, the average number of syllables in the generic class-noun phrases was 4.4.

I have chosen to begin with word and syllable counts for a reason. While counting syllables is a frequently employed statistical strategy in many areas of linguistics, tabulations of word counts have come under a great deal of scrutiny. In particular, what counts as a word? In areas such as child language acquisition, a different unit of measurement has come into play. It is from Brown 1973: 53ff that the mean length of utterance (MLU), a statistical strategy based upon the tabulation of morphemes in an utterance, originated. Brown sought to examine the correlation between age and length of utterance in children and, as such, this study is very different from that being undertaken here. However, the counting of morphemes is a further manner of collecting data on this particular corpus. In the corpus, the tabulation of individual morphemes was particularly difficult with names such as *dramamine* (<d(iphenhyd)ramine+ma), where the name is formed from several scientific components, and posed particular problems in counting minimal units of meaning. Yet, as will be noted in Section 6.2, such cases can be counted. In the corpus, the average number of morphemes per generic brand name was 2.1. In contract, the tabulation of the generic class-nouns resulted in an average of 3.2 morphemes.

5.4 H3 (The Process of Genericization)

> H3. Ellipsis of the common noun is a prerequisite for generic brand-name change. The process is ellipsis of the common noun which in turn results in a grammatic shift from proper adjective to proper noun. The next step is proper noun to common noun. The common noun then may become a verb.

This hypothesis is based on the belief that all generic change follows a prescribed pattern from proper adjective to proper noun through ellipsis of the generic noun. From that point, the brand undergoes both a semantic shift from

106

specific to generic and the loss of the majuscule shifting the noun from proper to common. Then grammatical change may alter the common noun to a verb and so forth. To test this hypothesis, a column in the table in Appendix A was dedicated to the grammatical categories occupied by each of the 100 brand names. It was assumed that an overwhelming number of the brands would be found to be generic nouns. It was also believed that there would be both adjectives and verbs as well. To demonstrate the hypothesis however, the presence or absence of a grammatical category in a given brand name would need to be considered. Namely, if for example adjectives appeared without a corresponding generic noun, we could deduce that the change was either an independent change from that of the process involving the change from proper adjective to noun or that the first change is not a change from proper adjective to proper noun but rather proper adjective-common adjective. This point will appear in again in Chapter 6. Similarly, if a verb is possible but not a noun this too would suggest a change outside the proposed process or the need for a revision of that process. Establishing the potential grammatical categories a brand name could be applied to was a task undertaken throughout the collection and establishment of the corpus. In the construction phase, where noted in the *OED*, the possible grammatical categories were listed. This was supplemented with information collected through the tokens of generic use which were employed to establish the genericization of a given brand. Finally, I employed native-speaker intuition to determine whether any other acceptable uses in alternative categories were possible.

The first examination was made to assure that all of the brand names in the corpus became nouns once the common class-noun was dropped. What was discovered was that 99 of the 100 brand names could become common nouns. The name which could not produce a common noun was *Day-Glo*, as in the sentence *?I'm looking for a day-glo.*[30] *Day-glo* appears to always be used as a

---

[30] The notational symbol '?' preceding a sentence denotes a sentence that is a possible sentence, but one that is not yet in use within the language.

common adjective (*day-glo*), suggesting that if a noun is not possible then the proper adjective has only one choice--to simply become a common adjective. Yet, from a single example it is very difficult to make such a claim. It does however bring up the question as to whether revision of the process presented in Chapter 4 (Figures 1 and 2) might be necessary.

While examining the brand names for eligibility as common nouns, a running count was made of those that were mass nouns versus those which were count nouns. In the count, 64 nouns were countable and 35 were mass nouns (excluding *Day-Glo* the total is 99). It is clear that both brand names for mass and count nouns can undergo genericization. Yet, neither appear to influence the occurrence of genericization.

Continuing with those brand names which can be used as not only common nouns, but also as verbs, we find that of the 99 that could be used as common nouns, 19 could also be utilized as verbs. In no case were verbs permitted without nouns also being permitted. Of the 19 brand names that could be used as verbs, the common trait was that these brands represented in some way an action; either through what the product does or through the extension of the action of applying something (e.g., to apply spackle --> to spackle). It should be noted that all of the brand names can be used attributively as adjectives. The relationship here between nouns and adjectives is quite close. It is worth pointing out however, that while in all cases where we found a noun we could also attributively produce an adjective, the reverse was not true with the *day-glo* example. Relying on a sole example is dangerous. As a result, we may wish to leave temporarily the confinements of the corpus and look for other brand names which might exhibit the same pattern (that of use as an adjective only). In re-examining the trademark checklist of the International Trademark Association, however, I have been unable to identify other tokens of this type. It could therefore simply be an anomaly. However, it should not be completely dismissed as it may still be of value, particularly in reexamining the process of genericization. Looking however at our sole example, one notable point regarding *day-glo* is that there is no tangible product. *Day-glo* holds trademarks for bright, fluorescent colors, and many products employ these colors. Yet, the colors themselves can be considered intangible.

5.5 H4 (The Single-Association Hypothesis)

> H4. There must be a psychological association between a brand name and a single product. It appears that brand names which represent items from a number of different classes are much more difficult to attach a generic meaning to. For example, the brand name *Tylenol* can be attached to any over-the-counter pain reliever (excluding aspirin), and is only associated with that purpose. Compare that to *Chanel* which makes a multitude of different products (perfume, clothing, etc.). In other words, a generic meaning cannot be assigned because there is no single item association to be made.

Hypothesis 4 centers on the concept that in many of the names that become generic there is an association with a single product. This is not pure coincidence; rather the hypothesis is based on the rationalization that for the product to become a generic we have to be able to apply the name to a specific product, as opposed to a wide range of diverse products. Simply saying that brand names referring to a single product are likely to become generic may be true, but many of the generic names in the corpus are applied to a diverse set of products. This is where the importance of the association is found. Let us examine a couple of examples: *cheez doodles* and *jockey shorts*. In the first case, *cheez doodles* are a single product, popular in its respective category. The association of the name is with a particularly-shaped cheese-flavored puff made by the Wise company. In contrast, Jockey produces not only men's boxer shorts, but also T-shirts, socks, athletic wear, and so forth. The association of the Jockey name however is to boxer shorts. Frequently, it is the first (original) product that a company produces that brings on the association with a single product. To demonstrate this, we can look at the example of *Tylenol*. Like its predecessor *aspirin* (a former brand name that has become generic), *Tylenol* is undergoing genericization. *Tylenol* as a pain reliever (either in tablet or capsule) was the original form of the product (acetaminophen) and the association was built from there. At present, *Tylenol* has a number of new products on the market, including acetaminophen in other products (cold formulas) in liquid form. Yet, when one asks for *a tylenol* the association is to a pill or capsule by McNeil (the maker of Tylenol) or perhaps an ibuprofen or ketoprofin pill, so long as it is a similar form of pain reliever. Form here should be taken quite literally and form appears to also play a particular role in genericization. What is it that makes a cheese puff a *cheez doodle* and not a *Cheeto*? The difference is the shape and texture. *Cheez doodles* are puffed and curved. *Cheetos* are harder and of a more abstract shape. This point came up again and again in examining the corpus. For a pot to be called a *crock pot* it has to bear the shape of a crock. An odd-brand personal stereo becomes a *walkman* because it bears the shape of a *Walkman*. In other words, they are easy to mistake for one another. A boom box cannot be a *walkman* despite the fact that we can walk with it and we can plug headphones into it. The shape and size matters. This too is important to the association with a single product.

To test Hypothesis 4 I return to the corpus once again. In this case, I will consider which products are associated with a single product and which are associated with multiple products. An important point must be noted here. Many of these products have been in the public domain for decades. New products come and go. When many of the products first appeared on the market they were the only products produced by the company. The addition of new lines of products bearing the same name was often a later development.

Turning now to the corpus, of the 100 generic brands 89 were associated with a single product. Of the 11 that could not be associated with a single product, several of these, such as *polaroid* and *xerox*, could refer to both the product and the output of that product (the picture in the case of *polaroid* and the copy in the case of *xerox*). In these cases, a single association remains however if we can assume that the output of a product can be named in the same way as the item that produced the output. *Ace bandage*, as another example, makes a variety of bandages of different sizes, but these bandages are in general much larger than what would by many be called a *band-aid* or adhesive bandage. The association to a single product remains intact however, as an *ace bandage* is any larger cloth or gauze bandage used to take care of an injury (as opposed to a simple cut on the finger).

This chapter has set out to test the four hypotheses while withholding discussion and analysis of the results of the tests. In Chapter 6, I will come back to the findings in order to determine the extent to which each of these hypotheses can be invalidated and whether further revision of the theory may be necessary.

CHAPTER VI. ANALYSIS AND DISCUSSION

"... The name of the song is called 'Haddocks' Eyes.'"
"Oh, that's the name of the song, is it?" Alice said, trying to feel interested.
"No, you don't understand," the Knight said, looking a little vexed.
"That's what the name is called. The name really is 'The Aged Aged Man.'"
"Then I ought to have said 'That's what the song is called'?" Alice corrected herself.
"No, you oughtn't: that's quite another thing! The song is called 'Ways and Means'" but that's only what it's called, you know!"
"Well, what is the song, then?" said Alice, who was by this time completely bewildered.
"I was coming to that," the Knight said. "The song really is 'A- sitting On A Gate': and the tune's my own invention."
-Lewis Carroll, (1872) Through the Looking-Glass

The intention of this chapter is to explore the results of each of the tests and to determine whether the hypotheses were supported by the data, or disconfirmed. If the hypotheses are found to be valid, this would suggest that generalizations can indeed be made regarding the process of brand names becoming generic. In Chapter 5 I sought to examine and test each of the hypotheses, and in that chapter the data were presented without comment. The restricting of comment was conducted as a means of permitting a more significant discussion to occur in this chapter. Therefore the layout of this chapter will consist of each of the four hypotheses being again treated separately, followed by a section on actuation of change, and the sectional conclusion of Chapters 4, 5, and 6. Throughout the chapter important statistical data will be charted, as relevant to the discussion.

6.1 H1 (Innovation)

> H1. If A is a brand name for an innovative product (one which did not exist before), then the association of that item with its name will become synonymous, rendering the brand name both a product name, and the name for the entire class.

Hypothesis 1 viewed innovation as a key factor in brand names becoming generic. I have long argued that an innovative product will require the creation of a new semantic class (e.g., Sections 4.3 and 5.2). It is important to clarify the concept of semantic class in branding as I have been using the term. The notion of the semantic class that I have been utilizing is one of multiple orders. Let us take for example the case of the *Hula Hoop*. *Hula Hoop* was the first product of its kind when it appeared on the market in the 1950's. The full name of this product is *Hula Hoop plastic hoop*. Being an innovative product, no class name existed. On some occasions, the suggestion has been made that the semantic class would be 'toys'. It is important to demonstrate why this assumption is misguided. While it is true that the *hula hoop* is a type of toy, the semantic level required by proprietary law is on a more restricted level than that of toys. According to the law, all brand names must be followed by a common generic class-noun. The class *toys*, in effect, is too general to serve as the class-noun. A sub-group is required, namely the kind of toy. There is then a hierarchy that can be demonstrated in the form of a tree.

Figure 7. The Semantic Hierarchy of Brand Names

In the case of the *Hula Hoop* and many other innovative products that are produced, no sub-group existed within the paradigm of toys. The necessity then for the company that produced the *Hula Hoop* was to devise a common class-noun to fill the then non-existent sub-category. This is where the expression *plastic hoops* comes in.[31] This was a devised mechanism whose sole purpose was to protect the brand, allowing it to become a proper adjective and protectable under the law. The problem for the company was that they were confronted with two names to deal with, only one of which would be marketed. In cases such as this, the fatal flaw that these companies have made has been in believing that marketing the brand name alone would be enough for consumers to learn the semantic class represented in the form of the common generic noun (phrase). This in effect rarely occurs. A simple examination of packaging shows the focus placed upon the brand, often through a larger font size, color, or design. The result then is the assumption on the part of the users of the product that the name represented by the brand is the name of the product itself. This runs contrary to what the law suggests as the purpose of the brand. As Patton (1980:2) argues, 'Legally, a trademark is supposed to identify the source, rather than the particular goods themselves'. The speakers of the language, however, remain in most cases

---

[31] Other types of plastic hoops also exist, but it is within this paradigm 'toys' that the expression did not exist prior to its introduction with Hula Hoop.

unaware of what is to them arbitrary information. The product is therefore learned in writing as *Hula Hoop* and eventually *hula hoop*, and not as a *plastic hoop*. Even when the name is learned as a brand name, this is no guarantee that people will not choose to employ it (the brand name) over the class-noun phrase. To elaborate this point, when asked about the nature of my research I often respond that I am working on brand names that have become part of the common language. The response is generally, 'Oh, you mean like *kleenex* and *hoover*'. The response suggests that in many cases people are aware of at least some of these brand names as brands, but continue to use them generically anyway. While written in lower case in the above example, it is the context of the discourse (rather than the loss of the majuscule), here the response to 'brand names that are part of the common language' with widely-recognized examples (*kleenex* and *hoover*) that tells us that people are aware of many names as brands, but also as generic class-nouns. Before turning to the tests for Hypothesis 1, one issue remains to be discussed. In the hula hoop example above, we saw the decapitalization from *Hula Hoop* to *hula hoop*. The issue then is, how does writing change what the object of linguistic investigation is seen to be? It is perhaps best to look at this issue in terms of the ways in which genericization can be determined in writing and speaking. As was alluded to in the *hula hoop* example, the loss of the majuscule is a key mechanism for determining genericization, and one that appears throughout this volume. However, it is not the sole measure of genericization. Context and grammatical form also can be determinate factors for genericization in the analysis of the written form. In speaking however, while genericization can be determined through context and grammar, we can not rely on capitalization (or lack thereof) as evidence. In other words, there is no pronunciation of the capital letters. So, how does this change our approach to the object of investigation, namely genericization? In essence, we need to temporarily distinguish our study of the written corpus from its application to speaking. For the purposes of our investigation, in this study we have been using a written corpus to establish genericization, and the analysis was based on this written information. This however, does not, and should not, exclude spoken considerations when applicable. The findings can not be divorced from the spoken language, as the two are inter-related (e.g., through reading). In brand names, I would argue that it is entirely possible to employ written data to account for, and alongside, occurrences in the spoken language. It has been noted often in this volume that one of the problems of the brand name is that it is not learned as the name of the maker of the product, but rather as the product itself. This is almost certainly accomplished as a result of use in the spoken language. This generic change will certainly be evident in the spoken language through the context and positioning in the grammar (e.g., use as a verb), yet it manifests itself in the writing through these considerations, and through the loss of the majuscule. As so little linguistic work has been done on brand names, I have deliberately chosen to work with a written corpus as a starting point. In particular, so much of the creation and proprietary status of the brand name is dependent upon the written form that to neglect this form of the brand, as pertaining to the changes that make up genericization, would be foolish. Further studies will extend this analysis and the results of this study toward the spoken use of these brand names.

We can now return to the data provided by the two tests conducted for Hypothesis 1.

In the first test run against the corpus, all of the brand names believed to be innovative in their respective classes were selected and tabulated. These were cross-checked against historical data where available. In the second run, the common class-nouns were examined. In cases where awkward or unusual class names appeared, these too were selected and checked to determine if they were primary to their respective categories. This second run may appear at first glance to be awkward; however, in examining the corpus this proved to be a valid technique. In the list of class-nouns it was very often apparent when a class name had existed prior to the brand. The example given in Section 5.2, of the class name *bandages*, as in *Ace bandages*, demonstrates this point. Dickson Consumer

Products (the makers of *Ace* bandages) certainly were not the creators of the first bandage. Often these names tended to be more general than those of the innovative products. To further this comparison, let us examine the class-nouns *motion sickness preparation* (Dramamine) or *flying disc* (Frisbee) vs. *wrenches* (Allen) and *pet food* (Cat Chow). The first two examples are quite specific when placed against the latter two. There is little doubt that *wrenches* and *pet food* existed prior to the introduction of these brands. It is unlikely however that the former two products existed in any formal context prior to their introduction as a brand. In the examination 50% of the brand names in the corpus were determined to be generic on the basis of innovation, or through a combination of innovation and factors covered in the other hypotheses. In other words, precisely half of the corpus (50) showed innovation as a factor in these names becoming generic. While one might expect to see a greater percentage of names exhibiting this trait, the other three hypotheses will account for many of the remaining names.

It is quite likely that innovation (along with a significant market presence and share) are the most significant factors involved in genericization. This can be seen when an innovative product comes onto the market. If we have no name for the class the product belongs to (what I have called a functional zero), the brand name of the first company to produce that product has little alternative but to become the generic class term. In practice, this occurs quite quickly. Among the recent brand names to have become generic as a result of innovation in recent years are *Rollerblade* and *Tamagotchi*[32], *and Walkman*.

---

[32] A Tamagotchi is a small egg-shaped electronic game, designed to mimic the life of a chick from birth to death. The purpose is for the owner to 'raise' and care for the virtual pet, or alternatively to get some insight into the tedious aspects of raising a child.

6.2 H2 (Length and Predominance)

H2. If the predominant brand name in a semantic class (e.g., types of over-the-counter pain killers) is shorter than the corresponding class-noun, that predominant brand name will become the generic for the entire semantic class.

The second hypothesis assumes that increased simplicity in market-leading brands will foster genericization. Frequently this is combined with innovation as well. Recalling Vandenburgh et al. 1984, they found that recall of brand names was best in shorter brand names (see Section 2.2). Turning first to name length based upon the number of words in the brand name and the common noun phrases, the results can be seen in Table 1.

Table 1. A Comparison of Name Length in Brand Names and their Class Names

Name Length (Words)	Generic Brand Names	Generic Class Names
Single-word names	57	21
Two-word names	42	54
Three-word names	1	18
Over three words	0	5
Average	1.4	2.0

In Table 1 the majority of brand names are single lexical items (57). This is followed by two-word names (42), with only a single brand name larger than two words when used generically. If we compare this to the generic class names, we can see a vast difference in the composition of the class names. In the class names, the majority of these names were two-word combinations (54). This was followed by single-word class names (21). Yet, it is also notable that where there was only a single brand name larger than two words in the generic names, in the class name category there are 23 class combinations. This would certainly suggest that the shorter names lend themselves quite readily to genericization. If we now return to the number of syllables per word tabulated in Chapter 5, this too will provide further evidence in support of this hypothesis. As with the number of words, the number of syllables per brand and class are tabled below.

Table 2. A Comparison of Syllable Counts in Generic Brand Names and their Common Class-Nouns

Syllable Count Table	Generic Brand Names	Class Names
Single syllable	5	4
Two syllables	44	13
Three syllable	41	20
Four syllables	9	16
Over four syllables	1	47
Average	2.6	4.4

The syllable count presented above shows the following: To begin, in the generic brand names found in the corpus 85 of the 100 brand names were either two or three syllable names. Only ten names were four syllables or larger. The remaining five names were monosyllabic. In clear contrast, within the constructed class names there is not only a greater distribution of percentages in class names, but also a higher percentage of large class names. In the class names, the largest percentage of names (47) were over four syllables. In fact, 63 of 100 names were four syllables or larger in the class names while only 10 brand names were of this type. Whereas the spread in word counts of 1.2 vs. 2.0 was not a large difference, when we actually break these names down into their syllable components we find some striking averages.

The average number of syllables in the generic brand names was 2.6 while that of the class names was 4.4. The broader spread can be explained by noting that many one- and two-word names were actually longer multisyllable words.

Turning now to the morpheme counts tabulated in Chapter 5, Table 3 shows the contrast between the generic brands and their class-nouns.

Table 3. A Comparison of Morpheme Counts in Generic Brand Names and their Common Class-Nouns

Morpheme Count Table	Generic Brand Names	Class Names
Single morpheme	15	6
Two morphemes	62	28
Three morphemes	20	27
Four morphemes	3	23
Over four morphemes	0	15
Average	2.1	3.2

Table 3 shows that here too the morpheme counts for generic brand names are lower on average than they are for class-nouns. The majority of generic brand names are concentrated in the area of one to three morphemes each. In the class names however, there is a much larger spread
with more than a third of the common class-nouns larger than three morphemes.

Before turning to the second part of Hypothesis 2, it should be noted that the counting of words, syllables, and morphemes was not in all cases clear-cut. In the counting of words, the treatment of compounds and hyphenated forms were an area of question. Are these forms to be treated as single words or separate forms? In the interest of uniformity, compounds were treated as single words (single lexical units), and hyphenated forms were treated as separate words. This uniform application was applied to both the generic brand names and to the generic class-nouns. The counting of syllables provided no significant problems, as the names were taken as a whole lexical unit, regardless of the number of words in the brand or class-noun (phrase). In contrast, the counting of morphemes proved to be the most difficult counting exercise. Many single word brand names were also made up of a single morpheme (e.g., *Frisbee*, *Lycra*). But, what of the more complex brand names? How do we count complex forms such as *dramamine* (<diphenhydramine). With the scientific names (of which *dramamine* is one) I chose to break the name by the visible minimal units of meaning (as opposed to further separations identifiable only by understanding the etymology of the name. In the case of *dramamine*, I chose to count the name as a single morpheme.

Primary market position has also been mentioned as a consideration. Primary market position simply means the number one product in its respective category (in terms of sales). With one known exception, all of these brands are the major players in their respective categories, and while it is possible that some of these names are no longer primary, the former position held by these names in the past is as significant as if they were the major brand today. Many of these brands can quite literally be said to be household names. And how did they become household names? Their popularity among consumers is certainly one major reason accounting for these brand names becoming generic.

I noted above that there was an exception to this primary position consideration. Finn 1993:66 reported that the brand name *Wite-Out*, while clearly being a generic brand name was holding only a 15% market share. The brand with the larger market share (estimated above 75%) was *Liquid Paper*. While some people may use *liquid paper* in the way they use the term *white out*, the latter is in far greater use. How can we account for such an occurrence? One way may be through chronological ordering, the more widely recognized product having been introduced first. Yet, another potential answer to this question is simply that *white out* is more descriptive of the action than is *liquid paper*. The name lends itself readily to both the action and the substance, and thus the verb phrase *to white out something* or *to white something out.*[33] To the users it would seem quite logical to employ the more descriptive of the two brands. This might suggest that while market share is important, semantic concerns play an important role as well.

A second question that arises now is whether it would be possible for two names in the same product class to become generic. I have alluded to this possibility with the example of *Wite-out* and *Liquid Paper* above. The answer to this question then would most certainly be yes. This can be explained in a number of ways. In some cases, different products in the same class may arise as dominant in different geographical areas and hence two generic brand names then would both be present in the language. Yet, in essence two or more generic brand names in the same class is not a problem for the language as these are simply accepted into the language as synonyms, similar to the many other synonymous forms found throughout the language.

It is apparent from Tables 1, 2, and 3 that the length of the brand name does indeed matter. In cases where a popular brand name is shorter or than the class name, the brand is likely to become the generic. After all, why would we want to say *correction fluid* when we can say *white out*?

6.3 H3 (The Process of Genericization)

H3. Ellipsis of the common noun is a prerequisite for generic brand-name change. The process is ellipsis of the common noun which in turn results in a grammatic shift from proper adjective to proper noun. The next step is proper noun to common noun. The common noun then may become a verb, etc.

---

[33] There may also potentially be a connection to the weather phenomenon called a 'white out'.

Hypothesis 3 assumes a regular process that brand names adhere to in becoming generic. This single process considers two variants to be in effect, one for change to a generic noun or verb, and one that accounts for a change to an adjective. This was first introduced in section 4.2 and appears again below in Figures 8 and 9.

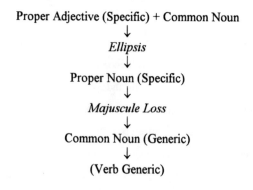

Figure 8. Hierarchy of Grammatical and Semantic Change in Brand Names (Excluding Adjectives)

Proper Adjective (Specific) + Common Noun
↓
Common Attributive Adjective (Generic)

Figure 9. Pattern of Generic Change to an Adjective

In both Figures 8 and 9 the general pattern is that of ellipsis of the common noun being the first step, which in turn triggers a grammatical change from proper adjective to a proper noun. Majuscule loss then occurs with repeated use and as a result of the loss in recognition of the name as a brand. In some cases however, we find that the proper adjective becomes a common attributive adjective only. An attempt has been made to account for this type of change in

Figure 9. In this case the proper adjective undergoes ellipsis of the common noun and majuscule loss. The resulting form is a common attributive adjective with no noun form, only a form that can attach to any semantically relevant common noun.

While these two patterns demonstrated in Figures 8 and 9 have been assumed to be the most likely pattern of change in genericization, additional alternatives have developed in the course of examining the corpus. The *Day-Glo* example, which can only become generic as a common attributive adjective, gave rise to the possibility that rather than being a separate change as demonstrated in the second process above, this type of change may simply be hierarchical, the change being a pre-cursor to the change to a generic noun. In other words, a single process is responsible for all of the changes encountered in the corpus. For this to occur however, the following process would be expected. The proper adjective, semantically specific, would become a common adjective, generic, probably through overuse out of the traditional context, extending the sense to objects with no connection to the company but which bear some psychological relationship in the minds of the users of the language. This step also assumes either a direct step to the generic common adjective with the loss of the majuscule and extension of sense, or that there is an intermediate step where the name remains a proper adjective, capitalized, but with an extended semantic range beyond the products made by Company X, the holder of the mark, before becoming generic. At this point the process appears entirely plausible. A major problem arises however when we try to proceed farther. If the process is hierarchical the loss of the majuscule must occur in order to give rise to the common generic adjective. Yet, this is where the problem arises. We know for example that we can have proper nouns after ellipsis, the brand functioning as a noun, capitalized, and still specific. In order to get to the next step, that of a proper noun, specific with the specific common noun phrase we would have to recapitalize and re-apply the specific common noun. This in reality is not feasible. English simply doesn't work this way. In a language where the users simplify the language rapidly through contractions, abbreviations, clipping, and phonetic short cuts this would be far too much work. This would suggest that the process must then be that as outlined in Figures 8 and 9. Yet, there remains one problem.

Apart from the sole example of *Day-Glo*, the remainder of the brand names in the corpus can be said to adhere to this process. 99 of the 100 brands could be used as generic common nouns. For genericization to occur this was entirely expected. Turning to those brand names which could also be employed as verbs, it was noted that 19 of the generic brands could be used as verbs. Furthermore, all of the brand names in the corpus could be used attributively as common generic adjectives. It is this last fact, that nouns are readily changed to attributive adjectives when preceding another noun, that poses a problem and suggests the possibility that these adjectives should be branching from the nouns and not from the proper adjectives. The process would then look like Figure 10.

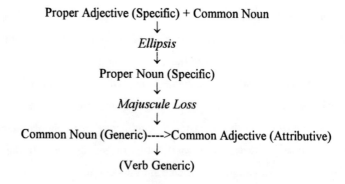

Proper Adjective (Specific) + Common Noun
↓
Ellipsis
↓
Proper Noun (Specific)
↓
Majuscule Loss
↓
Common Noun (Generic)---->Common Adjective (Attributive)
↓
(Verb Generic)

Figure 10. The Process of Genericization (Revised)

In Figure 10, rather than one process with two variants, we find a single process, where the change to an attributive adjective is simply treated as a function of the common noun. In the figure this is represented by a descending branch from the main process. At this point, a further re-analysis needs to be considered. Namely, how does the process of genericization function differently between speaking and writing? Figure 10 is set up to reflect the generic use of brand names in a written corpus. In speaking, a similar process is in effect, with one important difference. In writing, there are visual cues to suggest a generic use of the brand name. The loss of the majuscule is a primary means of identifying brand names being used generically. In speaking however, we cannot rely on such cues because capitalization is not articulated. In other words, we do not pronounce the majuscule. So how is it in speaking that we can understand a brand name that is being used generically? Figure 11 shows the process of genericization in speaking.

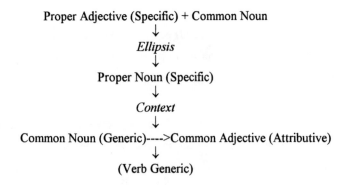

Figure 11. The Process of Genericization (Speaking)

In Figure 11 we can see that the major difference between generic use in speaking as opposed to writing is found in the greater importance that context plays in determining when someone is using a brand name generically versus when they are using the brand name specifically.

The re-analysis of the process of genericization resulting in Figure 10, and the clarification of genericization in writing versus speaking, has altered the original proposed generic process (represented in Figures 1 and 2 and again in

Figures 8 and 9). Yet, this re-analysis has had no effect on the experiments conducted under the previous assumptions. It does however, offer a more accurate representation of what is really taking place when genericization occurs. It is simply a modification of Hypothesis 3. The question which now arises is what to do with *Day-Glo*, which exists as a common adjective but not as a common noun. The likely solution to this problem is one of productivity. There would be nothing grammatically prohibiting Day-Glo from being used as a common noun. The other 99 brand names can be utilized in this way. Semantically, the meaning would have to be 'fluorescence'. It is entirely possible to create a sentence with *Day-Glo* as a common noun as in the following, *Even at night a day-glo resonated in the sky above the distant city.* While this is entirely possible, I am familiar with no actual occurrences of *Day-Glo* used in this way (other than that which I have just created). What in effect this means for the process is that there is an acceptable possibility for a noun to occur, but one which is not, at present, in use. This is not to say however, that it may not be in use in the future. This then is simply overlooked by the process, and the hypothesis holds.

Hypothesis 3 has assumed a process to which all brand names adhere. This has been demonstrated over the course of this book. In the cases of exceptions, these were considered and accounted for, and in some cases have instigated thought of the possible alternative constructions of the process. Nothing suggests that the type of changes found in genericization could be independent changes all arriving at the same point. Rather, these are clearly ordered changes, a process which begins with ellipsis of the class-noun (again this is often a functional zero) causing grammatical changes. In the midst of this process semantic broadening occurs, and finally further grammatical changes to a verb or attributive adjective may invoke.

6.4 H4 (The Single-Association Hypothesis)

H4. There must be a psychological association between a brand name and a single product. It appears that brand names which represent items from a number of different classes are much more difficult to attach a generic meaning to. For example, the brand name *Tylenol* can be attached to any over-the-counter pain reliever, and is only associated with that purpose. Compare that to *Chanel* which makes a multitude of different products (perfume, clothing, etc.). In other words, a generic meaning cannot be assigned because there is no single item association to be made.

The Single-Association Hypothesis recognizes the connection that the name has to the product the generic name represents. If we examine the corpus we find that 89 of the names in the corpus carry a single association within their appropriate semantic class, whether as a product (*Coke*), service (*Federal Express*), descriptive quality (*Day-Glo*), or component quality (*Teflon, Pyrex*). It is likely that visual aspects of the particular product also contribute to what the generic name may be used for. We can recall the *cheese doodles* vs. *cheetos* example from Chapter 5 to demonstrate this. Similarly, a *chap stick* then may be used to describe any similarly-shaped cyllandric tube of lip balm. While 89 of the brands were said to possess a single association, the remaining 11, when interpreted correctly, do so also. Many of these products do have multiple associations. The Allen Company for example makes a wide variety of wrenches of different physical sizes and measurements. This may seem to violate the hypothesis. It does not however. While it is entirely true that Allen makes a number of different wrenches *now*, the association is made to a single product in the Allen line, a design with a blunt hexagonal end on it used to turn some types of screws to assemble the parts of an item. Frequently we can account for this by noting that many of these products have been on the market, and thus a part of the language, for decades and often these products were the original product of the company which now produces a wide array of different products. Seeing the brand alone now could generate the false assumption of a multiple association when in reality the users of the language, through decades of use with a single type of item, make a single association to items matching the same basic description as what is perceived to be the item matching that name (whether it is of that company or not). The *allen wrench* is not the only such example in the corpus. We can see this again and again with examples ranging from *Levi's* (which makes a variety of different clothes now) to *Xerox* (which has now extended into computers).

That *Xerox* is noted above is important because it brings up an additional question regarding the 11 names with multiple associations. To use *xerox* as a noun, we can find that a *xerox* can refer to both a photocopier and a photocopy. The question then is why does this not violate the Single-Association Hypothesis. The answer to this question was alluded to in Section 5.5. As this occurs with examples such as *Xerox* and *Polaroid*, both of which involve the producer and the output, a further extension of the meaning has taken place. It then becomes possible to name the output the same as we have generically named the producer. This is not surprising if we look to other areas of naming for a similar pattern. Naming children after a parent (particularly the father) can be viewed in a similar way, the output or offspring being named the same as the producer. Sometimes the child may be named differently, but may still be referred to as for example, *a little Dan*, as in *He's just like his father, a little Dan*, particularly when bearing a resemblance or acting in a way characteristic of the parent.

These examples do not however negate the Single- Association Hypothesis. The association is first to the machine, and then to its output, a secondary extension of meaning. We can view this association as one association with two variants, the association being to the photocopier and secondarily to its output.

A further discovery was made in the data. Proprietary law mandates that a brand name is protectable in its class and any peripheral classes where a mistakable relationship might be assumed to exist. Just as it is possible for differing companies to apply the same brand name to products in two very different product classes (so long as no chance of infringement could occur), so too is it possible for two identical brand names of differing product classes to become generic. One such example showed up in the data. The name *Slim Jim* in the corpus is used to refer to a tool used by police to open locked car doors. It is used generically to refer to any such tool of roughly the same shape and size as the tool inserted into the window base to trip the lock. To many people however, a *slim jim* is a type of processed spiced beef that comes in a pencil-shaped stick. In my dialect, both types of *slim jim* are in wide use generically.[34] That it is possible for there to be two generic names that are of identical form does not however violate the Single-Association Hypothesis. Within their respective semantic classes there is indeed a single association between the name and type of product. This certainly supersedes any chance association between the two semantic classes covered by the *slim jim*. This should not be surprising to anyone, as homonyms exist throughout the language and rarely does the context not differentiate which form is in use. And that is the key that makes the two *slim jims* possible, they are simply homonyms referring to very different products, which are further distinguished by context.

This section has sought to examine both the effectiveness of the Single-Association Hypothesis and potential problems to the hypothesis. On the basis of the data provided by the corpus, each of the four hypotheses were shown to be utilized within the process of genericization. Problems such as the application of the same name to multiple products of the same company, secondary extensions, and homonyms have all been examined and subsequently explained in order to show how their presence is not contradictory to the hypotheses.

Before proceeding to the conclusions of these middle chapters, it is worth considering once again the question of the actuation of brand-name change.

---

[34] While both forms of *slim jim* are in generic use in my own dialect (Northern Midwestern), when I sought two independent examples on the Internet and in the *OED*, I was unable to clearly identify two examples. Therefore the second form of *slim jim* (the meat stick) was not included in the final version of the corpus.

6.5 The Question of Actuation in Brand Name Change

At points in the last three chapters I have touched upon the idea that amidst the problems of learning new brand names is that frequently they are unrecognized as such, the name of the producer of the product becoming the name of the product itself. As the assumption here is that this is frequently the case, then the actuation of this type of change is rather immediate; a combination of misguided marketing, unwary consumers, and the very creation of the brand name itself whose construction leads greatly to the semantic broadening that makes up genericization. It is, of course, at the completion of the change that we frequently realize that the change has occurred. This is one of the primary problems that the subject of actuation brings up. Grace 1997b has argued that linguistic change is instigated in a change in one's KOL (Section 2.3.1). This is precisely what happens when one acquires a new lexical item. Essentially, there is a change in the KOL resulting in a new entry into one's mental lexicon. If this lexical item is a brand name, yet is unrecognized as such, the result is the implementation, albeit unintentionally, of the brand as a common noun. The change in that individual speaker has thus taken place. If one speaker of the language can make this change then 10,000 can. Similarly, brand names are transmitted in the communication of individuals on a frequent basis. If the brand name is learned as the name of the product, then the transmission of that name to others will also be done generically and the change begins to spread. This is then the actuation of brand-name change. The time span for this change to begin then is almost immediate. It is because these brand names can change almost instantaneously that a clearer understanding of actuation is made possible. The question worth asking now is what can an understanding of the actuation of brand-name change contribute to the broader actuation of change in other areas of the language? Brand names are a rather controlled domain because of their restricted grammatical structure. Still, this study adds additional evidence for how one type of change in language is actuated, bringing us one step closer to a broader theory of language change.

Turning back to the statement by Weinreich et al. 1968:186 that all future studies will likely be after the fact, it is worth pointing out that it is possible to determine plausible avenues by which these changes may be actuated. This study has sought to do so by examining after-the-fact data in order to piece together the contributing factors leading to this one type of change, genericization.

6.6 Conclusions to Chapters 4, 5, and 6.

Chapters 4, 5, and 6 have been at the heart of the theory of genericization. In Chapter 4, I began by presenting the grammatical and semantic changes involved in genericization. This was followed by the formal presentation of the Theory of Genericization and a detailed description into the underpinnings, construction, and testing of the corpus. In Chapter 5, the theory was applied to the corpus of 100 generic brand names. This in turn led to Chapter 6 and an in-depth analysis of the results of the tests run against the corpus. The results of the tests support the four hypotheses with only slight modifications to Hypothesis 3 to better reflect the actual hierarchy of the changes involved in the process of genericization. Where counterexamples were found, these were noted and explained.

Before turning to the conclusion of this volume, it is important to consider how the findings of genericization in English might be cross-linguistic and whether any universal tendencies might exist. In order to start what will likely be a larger discussion in the future, I have chosen to look at a single language, Japanese. In Chapter 7, a discussion of brand names in Japanese, followed by an examination of how the hypotheses hold up against a language other than English will occur. If the hypotheses can not be disconfirmed against another language, it would provide the first evidence that brand names in very different languages do essentially the same thing, moving us closer to establishing a set of universal tendencies for brand names.

In Chapter 8 I will look into the proprietary considerations of brand names and how this book might affect the legal status of both particular brand names and of brand names in general. It is only then that it will be possible to offer constructive suggestions to companies about to embark on the process of selecting a brand name. As many suggestions have been made throughout the course of this book, these will be compiled together in Chapter 8.

The first six chapters of this volume have focused exclusively on English. We now move away from English to consider the validity of these four hypotheses for Japanese.

PART III: APPLICATIONS AND CONCLUSIONS

CHAPTER VII. AN APPLICATION OF THE THEORY TO JAPANESE

...I am once again reminded of the cultural nature of all human artifacts,
no matter how material they may appear. Inventions always arise out of a culture
and exist within that culture. Our understanding of technology must therefore
always be situated within our meager understanding of the nature of human
culture, to which language still provides the most reliable key.
-Mark Aronoff (1998:658).

7.1 Introduction

Advertising, as a medium of promotion of one's product or service is primarily conducted through language. It is through this language that the words used in the advertising are picked up by the public. The inclusion of this chapter, a chapter decidedly different from the others which are written with English as the example, is meant to expand the discussion to a non-Indo-European language. Its purpose is to set a precedent to establish whether the generalizations formulated and tested in the previous chapters may be applied beyond English. As the focus on brand names in this volume is on English, much of this section will consider how borrowed brand names behave in Japanese. Where appropriate native forms will also be utilized.

In Japan, frequently I found myself reciting the creative use of language emanated in advertising; singing the 'Pekoe song' from Suntory Pekoe Tea, or the

136

'Ichigo ga mitsu'[35] song which had three dancing strawberries (the play on words being the telephone number which was 15 15 15 (ichi go, ichi go, ichi go), homophonous with the three dancing strawberries (ichigo, ichigo, ichigo). I have long had interest in the effect advertising has on the Japanese language, and in particular, the role of one type of advertising, the brand name.

Before proceeding into the actual analysis of how brand names function in Japanese we must consider for a moment the etic versus emic approaches to anthropology and linguistics. The etic approach, long criticized in anthropology, has been quite effective in the study of language. Originally devised by Pike 1954 and updated in Headland, Pike, and Harris 1990 from phonetic and phonemic analyses in linguistics, the etic approach is defined by Salzmann as (1993:272), '...an analytical approach based on data that are verifiable objectively and applicable cross-culturally'. Contrastively, Salzmann defines the emic approach as '..an analytical approach that emphasizes units held to be significant and contrastive by members of a society (272).' In this study of brand names, I will be incorporating a combination of both approaches. This section of the study will be etic in the sense that the grammatical categories that make up the brand name (proper adjective and common noun) and the types of semantic change are believed to be predetermined and applicable cross-linguistically. Yet, the study will be emic to the extent that the uses of brand names by Japanese are individual to Japanese and these uses will need to be explained in relation to their significance to the Japanese.

Of further significance to this chapter are several linguistic concerns. First, this chapter sets out to examine what brand names, both borrowed brand names and to a lesser extent, native brand names, do in Japanese. Do they behave the same way as we find in English? Namely, do we find the same moves toward genericization in the same semantic domains as we do in English? Genericization here can be defined as the move from a specific referent of a given product, to the

---

[35] The Hepburn system of romanization will be applied throughout this chapter.

generic term for the entire class of products within that semantic domain. Brand names in Japanese, just as with English, are constructed of a proper adjective (the formally recognized trade name or *shohyoumei*) and a common generic class-noun or noun phrase (*shuruimei*). Theoretically, genericization and grammatical category jumping should occur in Japanese just as they do in many other languages. Therefore the first question is, do brand names behave in similar ways in Japanese to what has been found in English? While expecting to find similarities to English, one must recognize that there are some grammatical differences between Japanese and English. Such differences are important in that they may affect the process of genericization, create alternative categories of generic change, and may prohibit others. Beside the standard open categories of noun, verb, and adjective, Japanese has adjectival nouns (such as *kirei da* 'pretty' which cannot take subject or object marking, yet which can take nominal marking *kirei-sa* 'prettiness') and verbal nouns (such as *setsumei* 'explanation' which require the dummy verb *suru* in predication *setsumei suru* 'to explain', regular nouns cannot do this, **biiru suru* 'to beer'). While one would not expect to find a brand name jumping categories to become an adjectival noun, one would expect a normal process allowing a shift from proper adjective to noun as in *Ka ni sasareta, muhi aru no?* 'I was bitten by a mosquito, do you have any *muhi* (anti-itch cream)?' In this first example, the brand name *Muhi* (an anti-itch cream produced by the Ikeda Company) is a widely-recognized common noun used to refer to any lotion or ointment to stop itching. A second example of this phenomenon is evident in the following example using a borrowed brand name, *Bando eido* 'band aid' as in *Yubi kicchatta, bando eido choodai* 'I cut my finger, give me a band aid please'. This is a good example because the American brand name Band-aid (a proper adjective) was borrowed into Japanese and is being used as a noun, and furthermore can be used generically to refer to any type of small bandage. It should be noted here that there are probably few languages in the world which have borrowed so excessively in advertising from the English language as Japanese. Quite literally, the language of advertising is flooded with English borrowings. The reason for such borrowing is two-fold. First, the United States (as a major economic power) produces many of the world's major brands (*Coke, Levi's,* etc.). Second, the English language carries overt prestige in Japan. As such, giving an English name to a Japanese-made product is a valuable marketing tool.[36] As a result, many of the brand names presented in this chapter will be borrowed brand names that are a well-known part of the advertising landscape in Japan, some of which many Japanese themselves do not realize are foreign.

It should be likely also that one could find several brand names that have turned into verbal nouns. Shibatani (1991:217) notes *zerokkusu-suru* 'to photocopy' as one such instance.

A second question is, in what ways do brand names behave differently? I have noted above that there are some basic structural differences between Japanese and English. Are there certain semantic functions of brand names particular to Japanese? A further question similar to the previous one is, do native brand names behave differently from those of foreign brand names? One native example is *kuripu* 'Creap' coffee creamer which is in frequent use as a generic noun in Japanese. Another example is *kinchooru* 'Kinchoo' insecticide which is often used to refer to all bug sprays similar to the way *Raid* or *Black Flag* is in English. While these reflect the same processes as those found in English, are there others that are different? Are there new unexpected applications of the brand?

A primary hypothesis to this work is that brand names in all languages will move to generic forms given the appropriate circumstances. These circumstances have come in the form of the hypotheses that are the basis for the theory of genericization. Furthermore, while expecting similarity in the types of change

---

[36] This process of applying English names to Japanese products is often done in light of what may be also seen as Japanese nationalism or 'Buy Japanese' pride, the application of the 'Made in Japan' (Nihonsan or Kokunaisan) mark to the back of the product packaging.

between Japanese and English, the use of such brand names is expected to be language-specific. Finally, it is expected that by examining brand names being used in innovative ways that this will provide us with a clearer understanding of the influence that the language of advertising and commercialism is having on the broader language, namely the significant impact which is occurring.

7.2 Applications of the Theory to Japanese

If I may direct the discussion once again towards the work that has been done on brand names and similar domains of commercialism, this will provide a foundation for the body of this particular chapter. The American psychologist Friedman has done the most work on the influences of brand names on the language in English. In several individual studies culminating in a 1991 book Friedman noted a significant increase in the use of brand names in hit plays, novels, and by newspaper editors over varying thirty-year periods. These diachronic studies suggested that over time more and more brand names were being used in everyday language. My own work took a decidedly different approach. Clankie (1999) sought to identify some of the reasons brand names were moving from specific to generic. What was found was that in English, when a product is created, if the product is unique, that is the first one in its class, then that brand name, as it gains popularity, will begin to shift from specific to generic. This developed into Hypothesis 1 of the theory. It is important now to see how this particular hypothesis functions in Japanese. The application of the theory in this chapter, rather than being corpus-based, will focus solely on individual examples and if found, counterexamples, following the patterns of each of the hypotheses. Hypothesis 1 and its application to Japanese appear below.

140

product name	class name		product name	class name	
A	∅		A	→	A

Figure 12. Genericization as a Result of Innovation (Restated)

To summarize this formula once again, if a product A is created and there is no class term or the class term arises simultaneously with the brand name, then product A will become the class term (the generic) while retaining its specific name. To demonstrate using a Japanese example, when the Tamagotchi (see Footnote 32) came onto the market in the late 1990s it had no competition, nor did it have a previous class name. We can fill in the formula as above.

product name	class name	product name	class name
tamagotchi	∅	tamagotchi →	tamagotchi

Figure 13. Hypothesis 1 (Applied to Japanese)

Not having a class name, everything that was similar in shape and which exhibited the same purpose as 'a virtual pet' began to be called *a tamagotchi*. The real name of course is *Tamagotchi The original virtual reality pet* and while *The original virtual reality pet* arose and was created and printed on the package with the brand name, because it came out at the same time (and not previously) it may be treated as a zero. Worth mentioning here, the Japanese packaging for the *Tamagotchi* lists the common class-noun phrase in *English*, with no Japanese equivalent. Furthermore, the expression is semantically-complex, and even for many Americans this would be difficult to make sense of. As a result, many Japanese have simply ignored the English common class-noun phrase, simply referring to the item as a *Tamagotchi*. Evidence for the generic shift of this brand name, ironically, comes on the American packaging for the same product which appeared only roughly three months after the Japanese version. A slogan attached to the back of the packaging for the American version of the *Tamagotchi* states,

"If it's not an egg, it's not a Tamagotchi." Clearly this was a jab at the knock-off products (i.e., the *My Little Dinosaur* knock-off that was being called a *Tamagotchi* or *Daino-gotchi*). In other words, because of the innovation of the product, it is the name of the product which caught on, not the class name. Yet, regardless of whether the product is made by Bandai, or is a knock-off version, people will frequently call these *Tamagotchi*. Similarly, the lexical form *tamagotchi* has begun to take on new usages. As noted above, the *My Little Dinosaur* knock-off of the *tamagotchi* I have heard called a *daino-* or *daina-gotchi*, and the female who takes care of a *tamagotchi* is a *mamagotchi*. Another recent variant appearing in 2001 was the Tamao-tchi, a Tamagotchi which featured popular television personality Tamao Nakamura (instead of the standard chick). While the popularity for this product has already waned, it is interesting to see the impact it has had upon the language in a very short time, both in Japanese and in English, as it is generic in both languages. *Tamagotchi* is a single example, yet demonstrates well this type of change. A second example is that of *pokeberu* 'pager'. The word, from English *pocket bell*, was a brand name created by Sony to market its brand of pagers. The fashion of carrying pagers caught on in Japan rapidly (a precursor to widespread cell phone use) and subsequently the name for a prominent brand of pagers became the accepted name for all pagers.

Turning to the second hypothesis, that of brand length, it was apparent that in Japanese as with English, if the brand name was shorter than the class term, and if it was popular, then it would overtake the class term. This is evident when you have competing forms: an existing form and a new form, and one is easier to say than the other. In English, we have seen many such forms: *jello* (<JELL-O) instead of gelatin, *xerox* (<Xerox) instead of photocopier, and so forth. The simplest explanation for this is a communicative one. The Gricean maxim of quantity applies here in that we say no more than is necessary to be understood. Users of the language frequently take short-cuts to facilitate communication. The proliferation of abbreviated forms (*don't, can't, I'm, ain't*), acronyms (*NASA,*

NAFTA, ASAP), and condensed forms in speech (*hafta, wanna,* etc.) also typify such simplification. Similarly, Japanese is not without such moves toward simplification. *O.L.* (<office lady) instead of *hisho, pasokon* (<personal computer), *pokemon* (<pocket monster) and even in the grammar, the dual form of the potential *rareru* forms (*shaberareru* 'can chat', *taberareru* 'can eat') being reduced systematically to *reru* (*shabereru, tabereru*) are all for the convenience of the speaker. A figure for this rule is as follows.

product name	class name		product name	class name
a1	bb		a1 →	a1

Figure 14. Genericization by Simplicity (Restated)

Here once again in Figure 14 the a1 represents a given product name holding primary (1) market share which is simpler or shorter in articulation than the class name (here bb), the result being the product name moves to the generic position of the class name. This can be demonstrated with the following example.

product name	class name		product name	class name
kyupi	mayonezu		kyupi →	kyupi

Figure 15. Hypothesis 2 (Applied to Japanese)

Here, *kyupi* contains two syllables (and also two mora) while the class term *mayonezu* contains four syllables (and four mora). It has been suggested to me (by Emeritus Professor Takie Lebra) that Japanese is even more prolific in its readiness to shorten forms seen as redundant or unnecessary to the flow of communication than English. This is indeed likely to be the case, and if it is so, then it is quite likely that many of the class-nouns will simply be ignored, literally deemed unnecessary or redundant by the speakers of the language, if they are even aware of them at all. In effect, the use of the class nouns adds very little to the conversation.

These two findings suggest strong linguistic reasons for brand name infiltration into the language.

We can now examine what work has been done on Japanese brand names. Stanlaw 1992:66 is one of the few sources that mentions brand names in Japanese. He notes, 'In consumer societies product names readily enter everyday vocabulary.' He goes on to list four, *Shaapu* 'mechanical pencil' (<Eversharp), *Hotchikisu* 'stapler' (<inventor's name Hotchkiss), *kurakushon* 'car horn' (<Klaxon), and the now somewhat out of fashion term *ray ban* 'sunglasses' (<Ray Ban), all borrowed brand names from western products.

Similarly, Shibatani 1991:217 as noted above found some brand names (zerokkusu < xerox) to be borrowed and amalgamated to dummy (suru) verbs in Japanese.

Kotler and Armstrong 1997 in a survey of 9,000 Japanese speakers found the most recognized ten brand names in Japan were *Sony, National, Mecedes-Benz, Toyota, Takashimaya, Rolls-Royce, Seiko, Matsushita, Hitachi*, and *Suntory*. This study provides interesting data and backs up a recognizable and very important difference between the focus of commercialism in Japan and the United States, a point touched upon in Section 5.1. Notably, the most recognizable brand names in Japan were also company names, not names for single items. This is not surprising. Watching an hour of Japanese television commercials will reveal that less focus is placed upon the individual brand name in Japan. The focus however is frequently placed upon the company that produced it, and most commercials end this way. *It's a Sony*; *Sugoi, kantan, kimochi, Hitachi* 'Great, easy, feels good, Hitachi'; *Suntory no koto* 'By Suntory'; and other similar catch phrases and jingles remind the viewer not of the product itself, but of who makes it. The goal is clearly to establish not brand loyalty, but company loyalty. Contrastively, in America we frequently are unaware of who actually made the product. Few Americans for example will know that *Kleenex* is a product of Kimberly-Clark, or that *Dixie cups* are a product of the Fort James Corporation. This is an area rich in substance, and one which certainly warrants further research.

Takashi 1992 provides potentially the most interesting information on brand names. While primarily focused on language and identity in Japanese society, Takashi conducted a study of 506 Japanese television commercials and 413 print advertisements. In her study one of the primary concerns was the use of loanwords in advertising and the perceived effect on consumers. Charting her results she found that of 5,556 loanwords, 25.3% or 1,408 lexical items were brand names. This is quite a significant finding and will play a role in later discussion on the influence of these brand names. Other studies which are relevant to this one include Yanabu 1996 regarding a theory of translation, a theory which resembles quite closely the theory of generic change in brand names put forth.

Yanabu's Theory of Cultural Borrowing (1996)

Yanabu (1996:149) states,

> "In a narrow sense a can be a word in language "A". If a is exporting into another culture "B" that is different from A, a does not move into B as the same thing as the original a. It becomes c through the translation, then a' is not equal to a."

Yanabu's theory begins with language and turns to other cultural concerns. Our concern here however, is the expression of what is borrowed into a new language or culture which, though physically resembling the original, is in some way modified in the new language. This resembles strongly the extension of generic meaning in Hypothesis 1, but also is a strong characterization of what happens to loanwords in general. Here I would like to suggest a connection between change in brand names and the way that loanwords are altered in the borrowing language. The changes are quite similar and will be discussed later in this chapter. It is now time to turn the discussion to the linguistics of brand names in Japanese. This will then be followed by further examination of brand names in Japanese with Hypotheses 3 and 4, analysis and discussion, and some conclusions.

7.2.1 The Linguistics of Brand Names

Early on in my study of brand names in English it became apparent that for a brand name, any brand name, to be successful in its purpose as a marketing tool, the brand name must follow a particular format. As a name, the brand name however is unique from other types of names in two particular ways. First, as we recall, the brand name is a proprietary tool to mark one's product or service from that of a competitor and as such is regulated by proprietary law. This is significant because for a law to be effective on language there must be some form of uniformity applicable across industry. That is, the same rule must be effective for both products found in supermarkets and services rendered by financial institutions, and so forth. As such, this uniformity takes the form of grammatical uniformity. This brings us to the second point. Unlike personal names like John Smith, or Taro Oda, which are proper nouns, brand names are proper adjectives. Proper adjectives are modifiers of nouns. By law and by simple practicality, each brand name must be followed by a common noun. A survey of food packaging will show this to be the case for Japanese as with English. *House (brand) kare* 'curry', *Kikkoman shoyu* 'soy sauce', *Ajinomoto hondashi* 'a granulated soup base made from the Bonito fish' are just a sampling of those brands that can be encountered in the Japanese household. Without the common noun it is far too easy for the brand name to be taken over by other companies making similar products. The common grammatical structure of the brand name is quite advantageous to their study. It is so in that all brand names have the same starting point where only their date of creation varies. With all brand names beginning the same way, it becomes easier to see what types of changes can be identified in brand names.

The ways in which brand names can be altered are numerous, and not only involve semantic factors, but also phonological, orthographic, morphological, and grammatical changes. To begin to understand these changes, some understanding of the grammatical structure in Japanese is necessary. As noted above, brand names begin as proper adjectives modifying a common class-noun. This class-noun takes the semantic category or domain of the product itself, as in *House kare* 'curry', where curry is the *shuruimei*, or common class-noun. At this point we should pause for a moment to examine why brand names in Japanese should follow the precise patterning of brand names in English. The answer to this question is tied to the proprietary law regarding brand names. To this point I have referred specifically to U.S. trademark law (specifically the Lanham Act of 1946, Trademark Revision Act of 1988, and Federal Trademark Dilution Act of 1995) relevant to the construction and application of the brand name. Yet, American brand names also must adhere to international law if they hope to have any impact in the broader international marketplace. In effect, the purpose of the Trademark Revision Act of 1988 was not only to update the law, but to update it to the Madrid Protocol, a concerted effort by a number of countries to standardize international trademark law. Japan, while not yet a signatory to the treaty, adheres closely to the standardization in the registration procedures set forth in the protocol and thus, in the form of the brand name. Indeed they must adhere closely to convention if they are to register their products in other countries for exporting. Given this basic knowledge we can turn again to the first type of change, ellipsis. Ellipsis once again defined by McMahon (1994:184) 'results from the habitual contiguity of two forms; one ultimately drops, and the leftover stands for the whole string.' Thus with brand names in Japanese we frequently find *kyupi mayonezu* (<Kewpie mayonnaise) dropping the noun to become *kyupi*.[37] This in turn transforms what was a proper adjective into a proper noun and is the first step in the process laid out in Hypothesis 3. Ellipsis is an extremely important step here, because it has the tendency to set the other changes into motion. In other words, once ellipsis occurs and changes the proper adjective to a proper noun, then the proper noun can in turn change to a common noun, thereby changing to a generic referent of the entire semantic domain. This can be demonstrated in Figure 16.

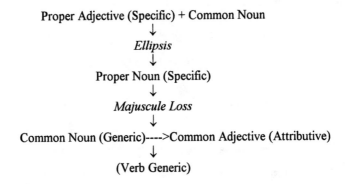

Figure 16. Hypothesis 3 (Restated)

While the process presented above is effective on English, some minor clarifications are needed to address the specific traits of Japanese. First, three of the four Japanese writing systems do not distinguish majuscules. It is only the romanized form of the language where one can capitalize. As a result of this difference, the separation that I have made between proper and common nouns is

---

[37] This is the same Kewpie name as that of the famous Kewpie doll. The doll is far more prevalent in Japan however. Yet, the precise relationship between the name, the doll, and the mayonaise has resulted in a trademark infringement suit between the U.S. holder of the Kewpie trademark and the company producing Kewpie in Japan.

less apparent in Japanese. Therefore, revision of the above analysis is necessary and appears in Figure 17.

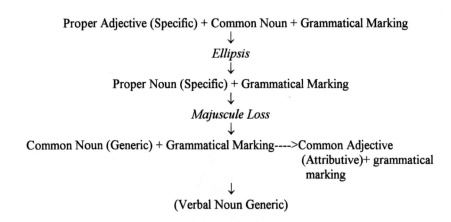

Figure 17. Hypothesis 3 (Modified to Japanese)

In addition to accounting for the failure to distinguish majuscules in Japanese, we should also modify the figure to show where the grammatical marking, or particles, appear.

Applying the process of Figure 17 to an actual example, in Figure 18 we can see how this process works.

proper adjective	proper noun	common noun generic
Tamagotchi	Tamagotchi (brand)	tamagotchi (all similar items)
		virtual reality pet

Figure 18. The Process of Genericization Applied to Japanese

Through ellipsis a number of changes are taking place, and it is likely that many of these are simultaneous in time. Yet, through ellipsis we can see not only a grammatical change, but orthographic, and often a subsequent semantic change, as evident in the example above.

While it is possible for a proper adjective to change from a proper adjective to a proper noun, it may also jump grammatical categories from a noun to a verb (verbal noun). We already saw one such example in *zerokkusu suru* 'to photocopy'. Other examples are *woshuretto suru* 'to use the toilet's spraying device'[38] and *fokasu suru* 'to chase people as the paparazzi do' (<Focus magazine).[39] While Japanese is particularly receptive in permitting brand names and other loanwords to attach to the dummy verb *suru* to form a verb phrase, it appears less receptive to allowing the foreign brand name to become a true verb (-ru form). There are exceptions however in common noun loanwords, as in *neguru* 'to neglect'(<neglect) and *saboru* 'to skip class'(<sabotage). However, no borrowed brand names were found to exhibit this type of change.

Similarly, it is possible just as it is with English for a generic brand to become an attributive adjective through both the loss of the majuscule in its orthography (if written in a romanized form) and the use as a generic without its common noun. One clear example of this was *zerokkusu janorisumu* 'journalistic plagiarism'. In this case, the meaning is of a reporter who gets his story from another reporter, newspaper, or television news program. Here the meaning has only a hint of the original sense of *Xerox* as a brand of photocopier, the analogy being made to the copying process. Here *zerokkusu* in *zerokkusu janorisumu* is nothing more than a common attributive adjective, a later development from the genericized use of the noun *zerokkusu*.

---

[38] Many modern Japanese toilets have a spray device (similar to a bidet) and dryer attached to them to clean users. This type of toilet is called a *woshuretto* 'Washlet' (>wash+toilet).

[39] Focus magazine, until 2001 was a popular magazine (now defunct) that had a notorious reputation in Japan for chasing anyone in the news (cf. The National Enquirer). This use of *focus* (in reference to paparazzi-like tactics) is the sole use of the word. To focus a camera in Japanese is *pinto o awaseru*.

150

The categories above of noun, verb, and adjective make up the open word classes and are particularly productive, allowing new forms to enter and disappear frequently in stark contrast to the closed categories of particle, pronouns, counters, and so forth. It is highly unlikely that a brand-name change will convert a brand name to, say, a particle, or for that matter, any of the closed classes. No evidence for change of this type was found in this examination of Japanese.

Phonological changes also occur, particularly among foreign brand names borrowed in Japanese. First, as Japanese is based on a basic CV syllable structure, brand names borrowed in Japanese will have their consonant clusters broken up so as to permit the lexical item to conform to the CV structure. Similarly, whereas English can have a consonant in the coda position of the syllable, Japanese in general only permits the voiced alveolar nasal /n/ as in Honda, or the first consonant in geminates (long consonants) *totta* 'he took', etc. Therefore, to adhere to the syllable structure further vowel adding will occur. This permits a coda consonant through the addition of a syllable-final vowel to become the onset of a CV syllable, thus preserving the syllable structure. To give an example, the restaurant name Kentucky Fried Chicken will become *kentaki furaido chikin*, where consonant clusters as in the fr- of fried are broken.

A further change taking place in the phonological altering of brand names occurs as a result of the timing system of the language. While English is a foot-timed language, Japanese uses an even more precise form of timing, mora timing, taking its form in the long and short vowel and consonant contrasts. Where a brand name such as Coca-Cola in English has four syllables (Co-ca Co-la), in Japanese it has five mora (ko-ka ko-o-ra) with additional vowel lengthening on the first syllable of cola.

The two types of phonological change noted above should not in any way be construed as exclusive to brand names borrowed into Japanese. In reality, all words borrowed into Japanese must conform phonologically to the system of the language (See description of *zerokkusu* in Section 1.3).

Finally, there is one other type of change not yet mentioned and that is what is commonly referred to as clipping. Clipping in language takes place much in the way that contractions do in English. A clipped form is one where part of the word is systematically dropped and the remaining part of the word retains the meaning of the whole. Examples of this arise frequently. An earlier example *shaapu*, or alternatively *shaapen* 'mechanical pencil' (<Eversharp) demonstrates this. The *Ever-* of *Eversharp* has been dropped, leaving *shaapu* while retaining the original meaning of mechanical pencil. The alternate form *shaapen* takes this clipping one step further by dropping both the *Ever-* and the final syllable of sharp (Japanese *-pu*), and then compounding to *pen*.

7.2.2 Changes in Borrowed Brand Names

There is a common lay misconception that when an item from one language is borrowed into another language, then that borrowed item will remain the same as it exists in the donor language. This is evident in listening to metalinguistic discussions by nonnative speakers of Japanese, who are bemused, and frequently confused, by unusual meanings attached to loanwords borrowed into Japanese. The simple fact is that once the loanword is borrowed into Japanese it begins to take on a life of its own. It may have started as an English word, but once it enters Japanese and is altered phonologically, then semantically, it frequently is no longer the same as it was in English. Additionally, it should be noted that language change is continuous. Words in time are under continuous pressures to modify according to the structural and cultural pressures upon the language. The Saussurean position on meaning here is particularly appropriate. To paraphrase Saussure (Lecture, July 4, 1911), meaning is an amorphous mass on which individual languages set boundaries. This is particularly relevant to borrowing because a given lexical item may have several meanings attached in one language. Yet, when that lexical item is borrowed into another language the

152

borrowing language will place specific constraints on the meaning attached to borrowed items. Rarely do all the senses attached to an individual item get borrowed. Once borrowed however, new senses can be readily attached to the new item. For this reason Stanlaw 1992:73 prefers to call loanwords or borrowings 'English-inspired vocabulary items'. While a good suggestion, it is misguided because it fails to distinguish true loanwords, which by their very nature originate in a donor language, from those loanwords which are homegrown English-like loanwords which look like English but which do not exist in the English language. To differentiate the two, let us consider two brand names found in most Japanese kitchens, *Saran Wrap* 'cellophane' and *Creap* 'creamer'. Both of these are brand names which appear to be from English, that is, both brands could be English words, and both are used generically in Japanese. Yet, whereas *Saran Wrap* is from English, *Creap* is Japanese.[40] The latter was created by a Japanese company in order to make it appear English. While Stanlaw would like all loanwords to be English-inspired vocabulary items, it seems that the true English-inspired vocabulary items are those in the latter class which are truly English-inspired. Other examples of brand names of this type include *Pocari Sweat* and *Calpis* (both soft drinks). The former class above (*Saran Wrap*) are simply etymologically English words.

Such brand names as those exhibited by the example of *Creap* have become particularly prevalent in Japanese, appearing in print ads, and frequently on t-shirts and other clothing items. There are a number of reasons why this type of English-inspired word occurs. The first reason is quite simple. Frequently, the copywriters are not particularly fluent in English and they make orthographic and grammatical errors. This accounts for a number of the peculiarities that can be found in borrowed forms in Japanese, but the question that one must ask is, Why is there a need for so many borrowings, and furthermore, why is there such a need

---

[40] The form of *Creap* used here should not be confused with the English verb 'to creep', which bears no semantic or etymological relationship to the English form.

to create their own words or brand names which look like English? This takes us to the heart of loanword theory, that is, why borrow?

There are several universal reasons for borrowing. First, and perhaps most frequent, are cultural borrowings. This type of borrowing occurs when some cultural entity is borrowed into a new language and the name of it in the original society is taken along. This would then include *booringu* for bowling, *hamubaagu* for hamburger, and so on. We could classify brand names borrowed into Japanese as cultural borrowings, as many of the brands introduce products not formerly known in Japan. *Seroteepu* 'scotch tape' (<Cello-tape), *koka koora* 'Coca-Cola', and *zemu kurippu* or *kurippu* 'paper clip' (<Gem Clip) are all brand names representing items not existing in Japan prior to their introduction by foreign companies. Yet, this is a bit messy because not all brand names introduce culturally new items. Often they are competing forms of an existing item. This brings us to the second type of borrowing, that based upon competing forms. The type is frequently found in brand names, with little sociological reason for borrowing. It is instigated by a foreign company introducing a product which competes with the local product of the same semantic domain. If the foreign brand gains in popularity and market share then that brand name may become a popular loanword brand, if not a generic for the entire class. There is no other reason for this type of borrowing than business competition.

Technological advancement contributes a great deal to the vocabulary of a given language. If a country adapts the technological advancements of another country, a large number of technological borrowings will infiltrate into the language. This frequently occurs in areas such as computer terminology. Brand names in these areas can become quite common generic items. Frequently, and with significant uniformity, an IBM-compatible computer will be called an *IBM* (ai bi emu), and an Apple-compatible computer a *Macintosh* or *Mac* (makintoshu or maku).

Additionally, there are a number of sociological and psychological reasons for borrowing to occur. The first of these is social stratification. Social stratification is the upward promotion of one's status by the words one chooses to use. In other words, the use of a particular foreign word brings positive prestige to the speaker, regardless of whether the hearer knows the meaning of that word. In the case of brand names this frequently takes the form of name-dropping, and what Tobin 1992 calls 'brand-consciousness'. Using brand names which carry overt prestige, as with purchasing the products themselves, brings this prestige to the speaker. *Chanel, Tiffany & Company, Louis Vuitton, Ferragamo, Ralph Lauren*, are just a sampling of the foreign brands carrying an eliteness and level of positive prestige popular with Japanese consumers. As status-consciousness in Japanese culture is particularly acute, when something becomes fashionable, causing a mania around the item (*Louis Vuitton* handbags, *Tamagotchi* virtual reality pets, and *Neo-print* photo stickers), the use of such words in speech brings a clear and positive effect to the speaker.

A second sociocultural reason for borrowing is newness. The use of a new foreign word is enticing to many speakers as a means of showing someone is with the times. In the case of brand names, the use of a new brand name in speech may show the speaker to be at the forefront of the latest fashion trends.

Pertinent to this discussion, and a reason which goes far further than the explanation I will discuss here, is the longing to sound cosmopolitan. Many speakers who wish to sound cosmopolitan or to sound as having a level of sophistication employ loanwords, and this brand-dropping is believed (by the speakers) to demonstrate some level of cosmopolitanness.

Finally, the use of foreign words may be perceived by the hearer as making the speaker sound more intelligent or better educated. The same feature may also make a speaker appear more urban, as it would be more likely that urban speakers would have exposure to foreign culture and brands than their rural counterparts.

It is worth pointing out that none of these sociocultural reasons are mutually exclusive. There is a great deal of overlap, and it is entirely possible that a speaker will use a loanword for any and all of the reasons mentioned above.

Turning briefly now to the linguistic ease with which Japanese permits borrowing, Shibatani (1991:144) notes,

> 'The main linguistic reasons have to do with a lack of nominal inflections and the presence of the syllabary writing system. Since Japanese does not mark gender, person, or number on nouns, and since cases are indicated by separate particles, a loanword can simply be inserted into any position where a native nominal might appear, with no morphological readjustment. For the borrowing of verbal expressions, Japanese utilizes the verb suru..' ... 'Adjectives are borrowed into the category of adjectival nominals..'

While the actual influence of brand names in Japanese may be empirically difficult to prove, there is little doubt that the impact is tremendous. Yet, some questions immediately arise about what can change and why. As we saw in English (Section 5.1.1), a number of the brand names were noted to be from the semantic domain of foodstuffs and kitchen materials. In Japanese, we find a similar situation. This moves us toward Hypothesis 4. Why for example do we find *saran rapu* 'Saran Wrap', *shi chikin* 'tuna' (<Chicken of the Sea tuna), *pokki* (Pocky chocolate sticks), and other items found in the kitchen changing to generic terms, but not areas such as high status brands such as *Chanel, Louis Vuitton, Kenzo* and so forth? There are a couple of reasons why some semantic domains genericize more frequently than others. In terms of the kitchen products mentioned above those brand names were single line products which either possessed the highest market share or were unique in some way. Contrastively, *Chanel, Louis Vuitton* and *Kenzo* all produce a wide variety of products. *Chanel* for example, produces jewelry, clothing, and perfume. *Kenzo* produces a wide variety of clothing items. It is the case that in Japanese, as in English, for a brand

name product to become a generic class term it must represent a single type of product alone. This brings us back to the fourth hypothesis.

> H4. There must be a psychological association between a brand name and a single product. It appears that brand names which represent items from a number of different classes are much more difficult to attach a generic meaning to. For example, the brand name *Tylenol* can be attached to any over-the-counter pain reliever (excluding aspirin), and is only associated with that purpose. Compare that to *Chanel* which makes a multitude of different products (perfume, clothing, etc.). In other words, a generic meaning cannot be assigned because there is no single item association to be made.

Figure 19. The Single Item Association Hypothesis (Restated)

It does not appear that the semantic class alone is a significant factor in determining which brand names become generic, so long as they are in the public domain. While *Chanel* and the others may not have become generic, there are items from this domain (let us call it clothing and accessories) which have in English become generic. *London Fog* immediately comes to mind in English as it can be employed to refer to any traditional beige or black trench coat. Yet, as the trench coat is the primary item produced by this company it has the ability, upon gaining the major market share to become the generic class term. A Japanese equivalent in this domain that has been suggested to me is *rikruuto sutsu* 'an interview-style navy Japanese business suit' (<Recruit suits).[41]

A question that directly arises out of this fourth hypothesis is whether social considerations play any role in which brand names will become generic, or are the reasons purely linguistic? From what has been discovered here, the primary social consideration of brand recognition or market share appears to be greatest. Yet, for change to occur the perception of the consumer must be that of a single item associated with the brand. It is only in this way that the brand can

---

[41] Recruit is a Japanese head-hunting firm.

become generic. Of course, there are also a number of linguistic factors that contribute to genericization, particularly in the case of competing forms as noted earlier. Those which are easier to articulate than the class term are likely to change. Similarly, when there is no existing class term (as the result of innovation or cultural borrowing) the brand name can easily become the class name.

While this section has primarily focused upon brand names that are loanwords from English, it should be noted that native brand names appear to follow the same patterns. *Kinchooru* 'bug spray', *saronpas* 'Salonpas', *muhi* 'anti-itch cream', *makiron* 'first aid spray', *pokeberu* 'pager' and so on have all become generic brand names. This remains an area for further investigation.

The discussion in this chapter has been restricted to a large extent to foreign brand names which have been genericized in Japanese. Yet, it is important to understand that borrowing is always bi-directional. The number of Japanese brand names in English that have become generic class terms has not yet been examined, however given the enormous and long-standing trade advantage Japan has had over the United States the number is likely to be considerable. *Walkman* for all types of hand-held stereo, *Nintendo* for all home video games are just a few. Cannon 1995:94 also notes the productive *Pac-Man* name, originally from a popular Japanese-made arcade game which has changed to a generic adjective as in *Pac-Man defense* and *Pac-Man strategy*. This is likely to be a rich area for further research.

Other areas for further study include a more accurate prediction of the daily number of brand names a consumer is exposed to by the various media and in daily life. These statistics would provide further evidence that brand names are proliferating into daily language in uses other than as specific brand names. The numbers I have provided in the first chapter were only speculative, yet I believe they are on the conservative side. Further research will bear this out.

It is evident that the role of brand names in the language of any capitalist country is likely to be greater than is realized by the speakers of the language. Much of the input from brand names is passive, purely visual data. It is however remembered, and over time, this information contributes to how we use the language (literally creating changes in one's KOL). As I have shown here, Japanese genericizes a large number of brand names in precisely the same way English does, and different from that originally intended by the company that created the brand name. It is unlikely that companies can do anything to change this as it is the price they pay for success. For the consumers, it provides an added benefit, a new word in the language and a new way of describing things.

It is clear that the evidence points to a universal process of genericization. Before approaching the conclusions to this study however, it is important to give brief consideration to the proprietary status afforded brand names. For Chapter 8 we will once again return our focus to English.

CHAPTER VIII. BRAND NAMES, PROPRIETARY LAW, AND LINGUISTICS

Linguistically, all modes of advertising now assume that the language is simply a resource, to be appropriated, abused, plundered or modified for any marketing purpose. This attitude to language derives from the profit motive, from anonymity and from the mass scale of advertising campaigns.
-Geoffrey Hughes, (1988:155) A Social History of the English Language.

8.1 Introduction

To many linguists, the subject of language as possessible property may seem far-fetched, yet it is precisely this that is taking place throughout many parts of the language. While the brand name is one area that has long been afforded protection under the law, other areas are, in increasing numbers, attaining similar levels of protection. Internet domain names such as *www.cnn.com* are being treated legally in a similar way to brand names (Clankie 2001). Attempts have even been made to restrict the commercial use of common nouns such as *champagne, sherry,* and even *catfish* (Time, 2002) so as to limit the ability of producers outside a given region to sell a product under that name. Increasingly entire strings, in the form of catch phrases, numeric sequences, slogans, and quite literally any expression deemed important, are being registered. To offer an astounding example, the number sequence *01-01-00* has been registered as the property of a single person. As a result of the registration, no other company is permitted to print the sequence on their products, lest they be accused of infringing upon the trademark of the owner. That a common language expression can be withdrawn from use for no other purpose than financial profit is, in my opinion, a far more criminal action than is another company actually using the mark in violation of the law. This chapter sets out to examine the phenomenon of trademark law, with particular relevance to how such legislation regulates brand names. This chapter is based roughly upon my original study of brand names (Clankie 1999), yet has been updated to reflect the current state of brand name regulation.

8.2 The Corporate and Legal Views of the Brand

The epigraph at the beginning of this chapter suggests the view of brand names held by most companies. It is a clear and deliberately protectionist one. The law regarding trademarks is known as the Trademark Act of 1946, or more commonly as the Lanham Act. Written in 1946, it was subsequently revised in 1988, and again in 1995 (in accordance with the Madrid Protocol). Oathout (1981:6) states that the intent of trademark laws worldwide is to 'protect a business from unfair competition and the public from imitations by means of a sign--the trademark (or colloquially, the 'brand')--that is unique to the particular business as the origin of the goods'. Trademarks also are supposed to protect consumers from being misled into buying something other than what they had expected. Yet the protectionist attitude reflected in the Oathout definition has extended to deliberate attempts to protect the brand name from becoming generic. This is done in a number of ways under the guise of 'trademark education'.

The International Trademark Association (1993), in a brochure directly aimed at writers and editors who misuse trademarks, lists five guidelines for the 'correct' use of trademarks:

> Trademarks are proper adjectives, capitalized, and
> should be followed by generic terms.
>
> Trademarks should never be pluralized.
>
> Trademarks should not be used in the possessive form
> unless the trademark itself is possessive.
>
> Trademarks are never verbs.
>
> Tradenames and trademarks are not the same.

A second type of trademark education comes in the form of the advertisements placed in writing trade magazines such as *Writer's Digest*. These advertisements typically call attention to the name, noting its status as a brand, and request 'correct' usage of the name according the rules outlined above, rules not devised on the basis of linguistic data, but rather by lawyers and businesses. A similar method has risen with the technological explosion occurring on the Internet, as several companies have now placed trademark education pages on their web sites.

As a major lobbying organization, the INTA heavily lobbies not only trade publications, editors, and writers, but also the lexicographers who compile dictionaries. In the case of a creative writer (literally anyone who writes for publication) breaking a rule, such as by using *Mace* as a verb in publication (e.g., *I maced the intruder.*), will likely result in a letter from the company pointing out the error and asking that the writer not make the same mistake again. These companies consider this one form of 'trademark education.' Companies such as *Day-Glo* even go so far as to provide a brochure to writers clarifying how to use the trademark 'correctly'. The explicit purpose of all of this is to allow the company to create a paper trail of their attempts to halt the semantic shift of the term in question from specific to generic. Such attempts are useful in court to represent the company's efforts to protect its name from becoming generic and thus falling into the public domain and into competitors' hands. In practical terms however, such efforts do very little to stop names from being generic. When a term does, to the point of becoming the class term, then the courts may strip the trademark protection from the company, throwing the term into play, at a potentially significant economic loss for the owners of the mark. The paper trail helps to avoid that from occurring. Companies have learned from the mistakes of the producers of *cellophane, aspirin, raisin bran,* and *cube steak* to name just a few, who have lost their trademarks and whose once-private names have come to represent the category of item rather than the product of one company. As noted at the onset of this book, the International Trademark Association even has a term for such loss, *genericide*.

With the legal and corporate side outlined here, the next section will examine this problem from an alternative perspective, that of linguistics.

8.3 Linguistics and Brand Misuse

While companies, lobbyists, and the law are utilitarian in their purpose, linguistics generally takes a more pragmatic view of genericization. In most cases, the subject has been simply viewed as common semantic broadening. In this section, it will be important to consider a linguistic reaction to both proprietary status, and to the efforts made by companies to 'educate' the public on what they consider to be proper use.

First, however, it is important to clarify some basic terminology. Throughout this section I have been using the word 'term' to refer to the brand. To use more suitable linguistic terminology, removing any biased connotation a brand name may have to the company who chose the name, these are lexical items. By lexical item, or lexeme, I refer to the abstract notion of word or phrase in its uninflected base form, which would typically appear as a part of the lexicon, or vocabulary, as represented in a dictionary (Matthews 1991:26). When referring to a lexeme, or dictionary form, I shall use the linguistic notational convention of using SMALL CAPITALS.

To begin, it is crucial that a clear representation of the meaning of the lexeme GENERIC, as it relates to the loss of the brand, be established. When legally does a brand shift from being simply the name of one company's product to become a generic referent for the entire class? Finn 1995:67 mentions several criteria by which a lexeme might be considered generic. These include listing in one or more dictionaries as a noun or without specifically noting that it's a trademark, or when, as discovered through a survey, large percentages of people cannot identify a brand as a trademark. Finn fails to make specific 'large percentages of people'. Such surveys at best provide little in the way of linguistic evidence. The questioning techniques are easily manipulated and, rather than surveying a sample from a variety of ethnic backgrounds, social classes, and dialects, may simply be aimed at one group, particularly those who may be less likely to have modified their language to such a change. These may include, for example, the elderly, whose language is less receptive to innovation. In at least one legal system (South Africa), the use of the survey for these purposes has been called into question. There, such survey evidence has been, on occasion, thrown out by the courts (Die Bergkelder vs. Delheim Wines Ltd. 1980(3)SA 1180(C)), as it has been deemed hearsay evidence and inadmissible (Webster no date). It is unclear whether South Africa's courts have come to a definitive conclusion on the status of such evidence. Webster (no date:6), however, makes this final statement regarding such surveys, 'In the vast majority of trade mark and passing-off cases the potential benefit of survey evidence is slight and certainly does not justify the considerable expense thereof'. Yet, the reference to the use of a dictionary is a clear step in the right direction towards establishing a definition for GENERIC.

Among the many purposes of a dictionary is to reflect accurately the language as it is used at a given point in time and to provide data as to the etymology of the form. As such, dictionaries have been a key in determining whether a brand name is being used only as a brand name or whether, as a lexeme, part of the lexicon of the language, it has begun to acquire new forms or uses (senses). The first criterion one may use as evidence that a trademark has become generic is its appearance as a noun or verb, in lowercase, or with alternate spellings. If we simply refer to a dictionary, we must recognize that dictionaries, though attempting to reflect synchronically the spoken and written languages as they exist, are imperfect and always outdated. Lexicographers frequently find themselves making judgments for the inclusion of a lexeme, or variant of a lexeme, in a dictionary. In terms of brand names, this poses a second problem. Dictionaries are being heavily lobbied to adhere to the rules for proper use. In some cases, the publishers of the dictionaries have been bought up by large conglomerates. Those brands which are under the umbrella of these conglomerates have been mysteriously overlooked by the dictionaries, a practice frowned upon by lexicographers such as Landau 1994:300ff. A result of these lobbying efforts is a disclaimer which now appears in most dictionaries stating that the editors of the dictionary make no claim as to the proprietary status of brand names included in their dictionary.

An alternative to this is simply to accept language as innovative and unmanageable as property. It is important to understand that the trademark becomes generic at the point where it becomes an acceptable alternative to the semantic class term, whether via a new grammatical category or through the application of a new sense to the trademark. As Friedman (1985:936) notes,

> Indeed, many students of linguistic change have adopted a functional
> perspective toward their subject matter, viewing new words and
> expressions as natural concomitants of social change that remain as long
> as people find them useful.

In spoken discourse, it is the speaker (through monitoring) and the hearer (through listening) who ultimately will determine whether the new use of the lexeme is acceptable, grammatically correct, and comprehensible. Similarly, in formal writing contexts, it is the reader and editor who will determine whether the sense applied to the lexical item is in accordance with the grammaticality and pragmatics of the language and whether the use of a particular word in context represents accurately the emotive and descriptive quality appropriate for that situation, not whether it is acceptable to the legal team of a particular company.

Companies place rules upon how the brand can be used, but are they overstepping their bounds? It seems irrational to attack individuals for misusing the brand. Corporate infringement for the purposes of financial gain is one issue, however individuals who are simply using the lexeme which most accurately reflects the item or service they are trying to refer to are doing so as a means of communication. Are the companies not at fault for failing to fully understand the linguistic variables which create genericization, focusing solely on marketing factors alone? And what of the companies, complaining to consumers to use the brand correctly while they themselves violate orthographic and morphological conventions of the language through purposeful misspellings and by altering the morpheme boundaries? It is clear that the only motivation for companies is a financial one.

Meanwhile, more and more of the language is being registered. After the Chicago Bulls won their third straight NBA Championship in 1993, they were not allowed to use what is probably the most accurate term for the event: *Three-peat* or *three-peat*, because it had been registered ahead of time by a coach from another team (by Pat Riley, at that time head coach of the Los Angeles Lakers). While this example is not one of a brand name per se, but rather a registered catch-phrase, it does show how the expansion of proprietary law continues. Extending the example further, such expansion of the law could lead some to pursue a policy of corporate warfare, registering phrases in the language that might be of use by a competitor. It is unlikely that companies can do anything to individual users of the language who are not infringing upon the mark for financial gain. Yet, they have succeeded in many arenas of the publishing world with increased pressure and threats of litigation.

The letter writing campaigns employed by these companies to convince writers to properly respect the proprietary status of the brand name may seem banal, however such applications of the law beyond corporate infringement verge on an extension by these companies to the status of copyrighting the name. In particular, companies view such unauthorized uses as a crime of writing, in line with other crimes of writing such as plagiarism, graffiti, and forgery.[42]

8.4 Directionality in Language Policy

Thus far, this chapter has examined the proprietary status granted to brand names and attempts to extend the law. Here, as this is a discussion of language policy, studies from language planning are relevant. In particular, the direction of policy must be considered and namely whether a top-down (government-imposed) approach or a bottom-up (grassroots or population-instigated) approach is more effective in influencing language policy (here, proprietary law) and what effect this directionality has on mandated language change. Fishman 1991:395 has suggested a bottom-up approach to reversing language loss. While this may not appear at first to be directly relevant to the subject of brand name language policy and genericization, a by-product of such discussion is that in many cultures where a hierarchical structure of a traditional kingdom or of chiefs exists, where only a top-down mandate has ever been realized, that a bottom-up approach may not be the most effective. If this is indeed the case, then the argument can be turned around. In democratic societies, where a strong bottom-up approach has always been in place (as with the U.S.), a significant amount of resentment towards

---

[42] Crimes of Writing is the title of a text by Susan Stewart 1991 and deals with issues of he law and crimes in writing such as graffiti, forgery, pornography and the like. The subject of plagiarism and the law is dealt with in Buranen and Roy's 1999, Perspectives on Plagiarism and Intellectual Property in a Post-Modern World.

prescriptivism, language police, language laws, and so forth will arise and the policy is destined to fail. In other words, the resentment comes as a result of what is perceived to be authoritarianism in light of democracy. In the case of the U.S., where such top-down policies are viewed with disdain (we need to look no farther than the attempted top-down regulations involving Ebonics and Title VII Bilingual Education), it is little wonder why greater success is not achieved in protecting brand names. It would likely take a concerted effort on the part of public, and specifically consumers, to feel a necessity to preserve the brand name for actual protection to occur. In effect, however, this will not happen. Most people simply do not recognize the value, monetary or other, that brand names possess. For these reasons, the trademark education campaigns of the INTA and others result in little more than the senseless scolding of unwary consumers.

8.5 Alternatives and a Possible Solution for Companies

Innovation within a language is a natural and necessary part of language development. The semantic shift in meaning from specific to generic, if anything, may be viewed as the ultimate accolade a company can receive. Their name is thus known by most consumers in a population. Yet companies, focused only upon the money to be made from a brand name, do not want to lose their trademarks. Criticizing the policies of these companies alone, without in turn offering alternative suggestions for companies which produce trademarks, would be to set a poor precedent. This study has sought to offer a better understanding of the process of genericization on the basis of linguistic research, as opposed to a marketing or legal treatise. As a result of this corpus-based study (as opposed to surveying and other techniques), several suggestions are in order which might assist companies in creating brand names that will avoid this problem. First, as has been demonstrated by Hypothesis 1, if one's product is an entirely new one with no class name, then some attention must be paid to the formulation of a class name, one with at least as much importance as the brand itself. This may not appear financially feasible, but is the alternative? Moreover, the class names must be reasonable in length and meaning. For what reason would someone wish to call *Velcro* by its class name (*hook and loop fastener*)? It is simply unreasonable to expect people to call it anything other than *velcro*.

A second point that companies should comprehend, and the focus of Hypothesis 2, is that if their brand name is more convenient, that is, shorter or easier to pronounce than the existing class term, they risk it becoming generic very quickly. We have seen many such examples (e.g., *Velcro*) throughout the data. As has been noted, such an observation should come as no surprise to native speakers. The proliferation of acronyms, such as *NASA*, *ASAP*, and of clipped forms, such as *copy* from *photocopy*, or *photo* from *photograph*, clearly demonstrates the point. Companies may wish to consider the class name and to create a longer trademark for their product.

Alternatively, companies could potentially name their products in a way that violates the phonotactics of the language, thereby making them more difficult to pronounce than the existing class name. This was one of the original examples, altered slightly, from my first paper on the subject (Clankie, 1999). One way of achieving a more difficult name is to use unacceptable consonant clusters or common clusters in positions not normally used in English. These clusters are difficult for many Americans to say. Yet, there is no reason that if the product was of a superior quality, it could not become popular. As one possibility, imagine that a new company creates a product never seen before. The company has created a class name, not too long to avoid fostering genericization, yet seeming representative of the product. For our purposes we will call the imaginary objects *ortos*. The company then chooses to name their new line *Ng ortos*. While it may be next-to-impossible for most native speakers of English to pronounce *Ng* outside of the coda position of a syllable (the most likely case would be speakers simply spelling it out as 'N-G' as in *One N-G ortos please*, or by adding a vowel making it *ing* or *eng*), there is little reason it could not become a success. There is little chance, however, that such a term could or would become the generic. In this example, I have deliberately created a class name that is short and easy to say. The imaginary brand, while being monosyllabic, would give most native speakers of American English problems (at least initially). It is unlikely however that companies would choose such a name. Companies want the brand name to slip off the tongue, to be easy to remember, and for everyone to use the name. Companies clearly want it both ways. They want the maximum success of the brand, but wish at the same time to restrict the use of the name beyond that sole product.

A third point to be noted is that companies often seek the most descriptive name permitted within the limits of the law. This type of name is extremely difficult to trademark. Yet, the potential financial gain causes many companies to pursue this path anyway. Companies need to be aware that the more descriptive the name is to the item for sale, the more likely the brand will truly become the name of the item, a casualty of genericization. If we return briefly to Section 5.1.2, I noted that 37 of the 100 names in the corpus were descriptive of the product being sold, and another 27 names in the corpus carried at least one attribute of the product in the name. In total, 64 of the 100 names pursued this path of making the name as descriptive as possible. From the data, we can see that a less descriptive name, while no guarantee of avoiding genericization, becomes generic far less frequently.

A further suggestion I would offer to companies worried about genericization is that if possible they might consider multiple products, rather than a single product. In practicality, this may not be feasible. Yet, as I have demonstrated in Hypothesis 4, the names of companies that produce a variety of products (*Sony, Christian Dior, Wedgewood*) rarely, if ever, become generic. Even if it is only possible to offer accessories for a single product, that could slow down the chances of a shift in meaning.

I have noted through the inclusion of a chapter on brand names in Japanese, the focus in Japanese society is very often on building company loyalty, loyalty to a line of products, rather than individual brands. American-style capitalism has created merger-mania, and with the exception of companies whose company name is also the brand name, very few people can name the company behind many brands. This is certainly to the detriment of many brands. Companies which stress brand and company loyalty generally build a returning customer base. We see this in a number of arenas, most particularly in cars. Slogans such as *'Built Ford tough'* focus on the company making the cars and not on the individual makes and models. This is also prevalent in the brand name specialty stores, particularly those selling clothing. *The Gap, Banana Republic,* and *Laura Ashley* all market a number of products under the company/store name. Department stores do this as well. We never find brand names such as *Sears* or *Liberty House* becoming generic. The reason is quite simple. We can't make the association to a single product. Stressing the company as the brand, or the company over the brand, will certainly shift the focus of importance away from the individual brand to the company that makes it. This may at first seem irrational, considering basic market principles of gaining the broadest visibility for a name. Yet rarely do companies make a single product (averting Hypothesis 4), and even though this may be contradictory to many marketers, the focus on the company has generally not been a problem for companies as we are simply replacing one name for another. Clearly far too much attention has been placed on construction of the brand alone.

The final suggestion I would like to offer is that companies recognize to a greater extent in the future that there is a pattern to brand-name change. In other words, we are dealing with a regular process. Consumers as users of the language are not to blame for the changes in one's brand. If anything, the companies can be seen to be as responsible, if not more so, than the consumers. They wish to have it both ways: maximum visibility and sales of the product, while restricting the use of the brand beyond the product produced by company X. It is too late for many companies with brands on the market already. Yet many of these companies will introduce new products and lines in the future. In addition, many new companies will develop in the future. For them, I summarize my suggestions below.

Table 4. Factors to Consider to Avoid Genericization

1. Consider the class name. If one does not exist, create a short, specific one.
2. Advertise the class name also, not solely the brand.
3. Brand names should be constructed with the class name in mind, and should be longer than the class name, or more difficult to say.
4. The more descriptive the brand, the more likely it will become generic.
5. Build company loyalty, over individual brand loyalty.
6. Use the company name instead of creating a new brand name.
7. Recognize that genericization is a process triggered by both linguistic and marketing forces.

One point here, genericization of the written form is a greater problem for the companies that produce the name, and the writers who use the name generically in print, than is genericization of the spoken word. While companies have sought to control genericization in the written form, they have done very little to police misuse in the spoken form. We do not for example, see ads on television or hear ads on the radio 'educating' us on the proper use of the brand name in the same way as those against such use that we find in print. The reasons against policing the spoken language are numerous: how to police the language, lack of permanancy in the nonrecorded use of the language, cost, etc. Genericization in one form will undoubtedly contribute to genericization in the other form.

While the major corporations, the counsels representing them, and the INTA take an active role to police writers and lexicographers for misuse to protect their brand names from becoming generic, for many companies the long term battle is over and it is only a matter of time before the legal system recognizes this. As Bolinger (1980:65) remarks on the subject of generic brand names, ' .. in the long run, the courts condone this, for they do not encourage private ownership of words of the English Language.' Language change and innovation in individual lexical items are natural, and in general, unmanageable once they are set into motion. They are however, to some extent, preventable.

Companies practicing trademark education demonstrate a deliberate attempt to mandate language as property, moving us ever closer to broader forms of censorship. Both companies and the legal system need to reconsider the purpose of brand names. While brand names likely preceded any legal mandate for their existence, the legal context for brand names was to protect consumers, not the companies. Twentieth-century capitalism has destroyed this principle, and it is one that has been lost in favor of greed.

In my article (Clankie, 1999:262) I made this final statement regarding brand names, a statement I stand by (with some modification).

> If we accept language as innovative, then we must acknowledge that lexical items are created and discarded by the population using the language. The need then to determine when a brand name becomes generic would be irrelevant. The lexical item would simply become generic once someone chooses to use it in an innovative way, governed only by the internal structure of the language itself. Of course this is what normally happens in language.

In reality it does take a spreading of the change beyond a single user to become fully generic. The principle, however, of language as an innovative and continuously changing entity is something that many nonlinguists (e.g., politicians, business people, and lawyers) simply do not comprehend. I am not suggesting that we abandon all proprietary law however. It is needed. Piracy and unscrupulous companies do exist, and some protection is needed for both the producers and for consumers. What I would like to offer is that the law does need to be adjusted to consider consumers to a greater extent than at present.

Companies can do something other than mandating language change. They can better plan their name creation, and this chapter is meant to support those companies desiring to create a better name.

CHAPTER IX. CONCLUSIONS AND AREAS OF FURTHER STUDY

> *"Don't stand chattering to yourself like that," Humpty Dumpty said,*
> *looking at her for the first time, "but tell me your name and your*
> *business."*
> *"My name is Alice, but -"*
> *"It's a stupid name enough!" Humpty Dumpty interrupted impatiently.*
> *"What does it mean?"*
> *"Must a name mean something?" Alice asked doubtfully.*
> *"Of course it must," Humpty Dumpty said with a short laugh: "my name*
> *means the shape I am - and a good handsome shape it is, too. With a*
> *name like yours you might be any shape, almost."*
> *"Why do you sit out here all alone?" said Alice, not wishing to begin an*
> *argument.*
>   -Lewis Carroll, (1872) Through the Looking-Glass

9.1 Conclusions

The purpose of this book has been twofold. First, I sought to present the four hypotheses that make up the theory of genericization. In doing so, I have created a corpus from which other scholars will be able to draw information for additional studies on the subject. To summarize these four hypotheses, Hypothesis 1 dealt with the creation and use of the common nouns that are initially modified by the brand. Hypothesis 2 considered the importance of length of the brand versus the class-noun. Both of these hypotheses suggested that shorter brand names, particularly those shorter than their class-nouns, or those which represent a new or previously nonexistent class, were likely candidates for genericization. Hypothesis 3 viewed genericization as a regular, patterned, and hierarchical process. This hypothesis was the only one of the four to require modification, in this case to more accurately demonstrate the shift to adjectival status from the noun. In Chapter 6, Hypothesis 3 was altered. Yet, this did little damage to the overall theory, as Hypothesis 3 simply argues for a process which begins with ellipsis, and this is indeed what occurs. Finally, Hypothesis 4 sought to explain more clearly why some brands become generic while others do not. It showed that there was a greater likelihood for genericization to occur in brand names representing a single identifiable product as opposed to those used for a line of varying products, as one of the most important conditions for genericization to occur is association with a single product. Each of the four hypotheses was explained and tested, and counterevidence was sought. In each case the hypotheses were shown to explain how genericization is triggered in brand names--that this is not simply a result of successful marketing, but that genericization is triggered by linguistic, in addition to social, variables. The analysis described in Chapter 6 then attempted to account more accurately for why brand names become generic.

In Chapter 7, I sought to test the theory against a non-Indo-European language. As in English, Japanese brand names followed precisely the same pattern. A major difference between the two societies, however, is the focus on company loyalty over individual brand loyalty in Japan. This has resulted in genericization being less of a problem in Japan with many multi-product lines under the same brand. The result is that these brands fail to satisfy Hypothesis 4 (The Single-Association Hypothesis) and thus avoid genericization.

The second purpose of this study was explained in Chapter 8, where I briefly considered the legal and proprietary status of brand names and proposed a set of criteria by which companies might produce a better brand name in the future. Once genericization is recognized to occur on the basis of linguistic traits (in addition to those based on market share), it is then possible to suggest ways to build a better brand name. I ended Chapter 8 with a list of considerations to assist those wishing to build a better brand name.

In Chapter 1, I set out a number of questions that the theory would attempt to answer. We can now return to those questions and briefly touch upon what has been discovered. The first question was whether certain semantic classes change more easily than others. As long as the names are in the public domain, genericization can occur. From the data we can see that food items were most frequently present in the corpus, yet this does not suggest that food items are linguistically more likely than bathroom cleaners, or toys, to become generic. Rather, food plays such a central role in our lives, and we are confronted with new products to such an extent, that genericization manifests itself more frequently within this domain. A second question was whether certain phonological considerations contribute to generic change. As was alluded to by Hypothesis 2, the length of both the brand name and the generic class-noun do indeed have an effect on which names will be apt to change.

Two additional questions focused on the factors contributing to generic change, and whether the reasons for such change are purely linguistic. We have seen throughout this book that both linguistic and nonlinguistic factors contribute to genericization. Length was just mentioned, but also use in speaking versus writing, spread of generic use, novelty, market share, exposure in the marketplace, how the product is marketed, and several other factors affect genericization.

Another question centered on whether genericization is a regular process. The answer to this question, alluded to throughout the book, is Yes. Hypothesis 3 set out to illustrate this process. As it was discussed above, further discussion would be redundant.

Many of the questions in Chapter 1 were dealt with over the course of the individual chapters and will not be re-addressed here. Still, I would like to return for a moment to one final question, namely; what does it mean to 'misuse' language? For example, am I misusing the language by using *xerox* as a verb? Clearly not. I am simply using what I feel is the most descriptive expression for the meaning I am trying to convey. Grammatical rules in language, particularly prescriptive rules (those which are matters of performance), are frequently altered, and are many times ignored by those who use the language. Why should the use of brand names be any different? Misuse is a notion placed upon the language through prescriptive views of what is perceived to be right. And who determines what is right? It is the users of the language who will determine what is grammatical and acceptable, not the legal counsels of a particular company, regardless of proprietary law.

A number of discoveries were made during the course of this study. In Clankie 1999 I alluded to the ideas that have become Hypotheses 1 and 2. In this volume these hypotheses were more formally explained. Hypothesis 4 was discovered during the preliminary research for Chapter 7 and is vital to understanding one significant reason why some brand names become generic while others do not. I believe however, that it is Hypothesis 3, the process of genericization, that is the most significant finding in this work. Entering this research I believed that there was a process of generic brand-name change at work, yet I was relatively unaware of what it was, and of what changes were possible. What I found was that generic change is regular. This is a new finding in my work. A further finding of this research was the differentiation of Type 1 and Type 2 changes in genericization. Additional findings include the discovery of the contributing factors to generic brand-name change. These contributing factors were charted out in Chapter 8 for companies seeking to create a better brand name. Finally, I have gained a much fuller appreciation of what the study of names and naming practices can contribute to both linguistic, and more broadly, to cultural research.

This work has provided me with a greater understanding of the processes and relationships involved in the creation of brand names. Discovering the changes (grammatical, semantic, and other changes) forming genericization was no easy task. The creation of a corpus from which to consider the possibilities made the identification of this process possible. The relationship between the semantic and grammatical changes involved in this type of naming was particularly enlightening. Further studies in the future will bring new evidence to bear on this type of change.

9.2 Weaknesses and Areas of Further Study

In this study, a great deal of care was taken to identify, list, classify, and analyze the 100 brand names making up the corpus (See Sections 4.4.1 and 5.1). This was done through the identification of brands considered generic by other researchers. Yet, this accounted for only roughly 2/3 (61) of the corpus. As a result, it was necessary for me to select the remaining 1/3 (39) of the corpus, cross-checked against examples from the Internet. Ideally, and for absolute objectivity, the entire corpus would have been identified by other researchers, leaving me to solely concentrate on whether they were indeed generic, then testing the theory against these names. Despite my attempts to select only brand names previously noted and those still registered, five of the brand names included (both from my selection and those of other authors) were no longer registered brands, having already succumbed to genericization. These problems were all believed to be minor ones that did little more than slow down the data collection and analysis.

A theoretical weakness of this work was in the establishment of genericization. I depended on two verifiable tokens of each brand name in a generic context (usually through the loss of the majuscule and/or context). This is far less than I would have preferred. However, given a corpus of 100, two tokens each resulted in 200 examples (See Appendix B). With the addition of one or two additional tokens per brand, the amount of background work (identification, recording, analysis, etc.) solely for the creation of the corpus increases tremendously, each multiple increasing the corpus by 100 tokens. This was simply not feasible, and thus the number two was settled upon. Yet, with the current corpus established, further work on the corpus, both by other researchers and by me, can contribute to increasing the size of the corpus, both in terms of entries and of sample tokens.

An additional problem with the corpus is that it is solely comprised of generic brand names. Further work on this corpus should include a random selection of non-generic brand names that may be used for comparison against the generic brand names.

One final weakness of this work is that no two speakers (or in this case, writers) are going to use the language in precisely the same way. As a result, readers of this work may find that in their own particular idiolect some of these brands simply are not (yet) generic. This has been a traditional problem in linguistics (particularly in grammaticality judgments in syntax) and not simply in this work. Genericization may therefore differ from one individual to the next. This is not a problem if genericization is viewed as a process, a continuum with brand names at varying stages both collectively in the society and among individuals. It is hoped that the theory will hold, despite the possibility that individual brand names may be seen, by some, not to be generic. It is believed however, that all 100 of these brands can be and are being used generically.

I turn now to areas for further research. First, greater counterevidence is sought against the hypotheses presented in this volume. Where found in the data of this study, these were accounted for and explained. Moreover, additional studies are needed on brands in other languages to see if these tendencies are universal. The inclusion of a chapter on brand names in Japanese suggests that the same rules apply. Second, greater consideration is needed toward how brand-name change is related to the types of change witnessed in other types of names which become acceptable as common nouns, particularly in areas such as personal names and toponyms.

An additional area for further study is what I have identified as Type 2 changes, those changes involving semantic changes which bear no relationship to the class terms (e.g., e-mail *spam*). This type of semantic change would be interesting to examine in light of the results of this present study.

The corpus used in this study has established a foundation based upon a written corpus. Later studies will also focus to a greater extent upon the use of generic brand names in the spoken language.

As a final word, brand names are present in many aspects of everyday life. That relatively little has been done linguistically in the area is unusual. This book is the first study of its kind on this type of change. It is hoped that it will not be the last. To end in the same way we began, our character, at the end of the day turns off his Sony television, enters the bathroom and brushes his teeth with *Crest* toothpaste, then goes into the bedroom and switches on the alarm on his *Seiko* clock. He then turns out the light and climbs in between the *Ralph Lauren* sheets on his bed, kissing his wife good night, before closing his eyes for a well-deserved night's sleep. It has been a long day.

APPENDIX A. CORPUS OF GENERIC BRAND NAMES

Generic name	Full Name	Producer	Grammar	Source
1. ace bandage	Ace elastic bandage	Becton Dickinson Consumer Products	N, A	
2. allen wrench	Allen wrenches	Allen Co.	N, A	
3. astroturf	AstroTurf synthetic turf	Southwestern Regional Ind.	N, V, A	Donlan
4. baggies	Baggies plastic bag	Tenneco	N, A	Lederer
5. bake-off, Bake-off, or bake off	Bake-Off cooking and baking contests	Pillsbury	N, V, A	WD 12/94
6. band-aid or band aid	Band-Aid adhesive bandages	Johnson & Johnson	N, V, A	
7 ben-gay or bengay	Ben-Gay analgesic ointment	Pfizer	N, A	
8. bondo	Bondo body filler	Bondo-Marhyde	N, V, A	
9. brasso	Brasso polish for brash	Reckitt & Colman Inc.	N, A	
10. brillo pad	Brillo scouring pads	Purex Corp.	N, A	Lederer
11. cat chow	Cat Chow pet food	Purina	N, A	
12. chap stick, chapstick	Chap Stick lip balm	A. H. Robins Inc.	N, V, A	Lederer
13. cheese doodles	Cheez Doodles cheese flavored puffs	Wise	N, A	
14. cheese whiz	Cheez Whiz processed cheese spread	Kraft	N, A	
15. coke, coca-cola	Coke soft drinks	The Coca-Cola Co.	N, A	Donlan

16. cool whip	Cool Whip dessert topping	Kraft	N, A	
17. crayolas	Crayola crayons	Binney & Smith	N, A	WD 3/94
18. crock pot	Crock-Pot electric casseroles	Rival	N, A	Adams
19. dacron	Dacron polyester fiber	Du Pont	N, A	
20. day-glo, dayglo, dayglow, day glow	Day-Glo daylight fluorescent colors	Day-Glo Color Corporation	A	
21. dictaphone	Dictaphone voice processing products	Dictaphone Corp.	N, A	
22. dixie cup	Dixie paper cups	Fort James Corp.	N, A	Lederer
23. dramamine	Dramamine motion sickness preparation	Prarmacia-UpJohn	N, A	Adams
24. drano, draino	Drano drain opener	Johnson Wax	N, A	
25. dumpster	Dumpster trash containers	Dempster Systems, Inc.	N, A	Triplett
26. federal express, fedex	Federal Express overnight delivery services	FedEx Corp.	N, V, A	Donlan
27. fiberglass, fibreglass, fibre-glass, fiber-glass	Fiberglas yarns, fibers, insulation	Owens-Corning	N, A	Donlan
28. fig newtons	Fig Newton cookies	Nabisco	N, A	
29. formica	Formica laminated plastics	Formica Corp.	N, A	WD 6/98

30 freon	Freon refrigerant	Du Pont	N, A	
31. frigidaire	Frigidair appliances	White Consolidated	N, A	WD 11/97
32. frisbee, frisby	Frisbee flying discs	Wham-O Manufactur-ing Company	N, A	Donlan
33. gore-tex, goretex	Gore-Tex water repellant fabric	W. L. Gore & Associates	N, A	WD 9/97
34. hi-liter, highlighter	Hi-Liter highlighting markers	Avery	N, A	
35. hovercraft	Hovercraft sea transport vessels	Saunders Roe	N, V, A	
36. hula hoop	Hula Hoop plastic hoops	Marlex	N, V, A	
37. jacuzzi	Jacuzzi whirlpool baths	Jacuzzi Inc.	N, A	Adams
38. jeep	Jeep all-terrain vehicles	Chrysler	N, V, A	Donlan
39. jello	Jell-O	Kraft	N, A	Lederer
40. jockey shorts	Jockey underwear	Jockey International	N, A	Lederer
41. kitty litter	Kitty Litter cat box filler	Lowe's Inc.	N, A	Donlan
42. kleenex	Kleenex tissues	Kimberly-Clark Corp.	N, A	WD 3/98
43. kool-aid, kool aid or koolaide	Kool-Aid soft drink mixes	Kraft	N, A	
44. laundromat	Laundromat self-service laundries	White Consolidated Industries	N, A	Donlan
45. levi's, levis	Levi's jeans	Levi-Strauss	N, A	Lederer
46. lifesavers	Life Savers candy	Nabisco	N, A	

47. lycra	Lycra spandex fibers	Du Pont	N, A	WD 9/94
48. mace	Mace tear gas	Mace Corp.	N, V, A	Triplett
49. magic marker	Magic Marker nylon tipped writing instruments	Binney & Smith	N, A	WD 3/94
50. milk-bone, milk bone	Milk-Bone dog biscuits	Nabisco	N, A	
51. muzak	Muzak background music systems	Muzak Limited Partnership	N, A	
52. novocaine	Novocain local anesthetic	H. A. Metz Laboratories	N, A	Lederer
53. nutrasweet, nutrisweet	NutraSweet sweetener	The NutraSweet Company	N, A	WD 6/94
54. pine sol, pinesol	Pine Sol disinfectant cleaner	The Clorox Company	N, A	
55. ping-pong, ping pong	Ping-Pong table tennis equipment	Parker Brothers	N, A	Lederer
56. plexiglass	Plexiglas acrylic plastic	Roam and Haas Company	N, A	Triplett
57. polaroid	Polaroid cameras, film	Polaroid Corp.	N, A	
58. pop-tarts, pop tarts	Pop-Tarts toaster pastry	Kellogg's	N, A	Lederer
59 porta potty, porta-potty	Porta Potti portable toilets	Thetford	N, A	
60. post-it notes, post it notes	Post-it self stick notes	3M	N, A	WD 6/98
61. pyrex	Pyrex brand glassware	Corning	N, A	

62. q-tip	Q-Tips cotton swabs	Cheesebo-rough-Ponds	N, A	
63. real lemon	ReaLemon lemon juice concentrate	Borden	N, A	
64. realtor	Realtor real estate broker, member of National Association of Realtors	National Association of Realtors	N, A	Triplett
65. rice crispies, rice krispies, Rice Crispy	Rice Krispies cereal	Kellogg's	N, A	
66. rollerblades	Rollerblade in-line skates	Rollerblade Inc.	N, V, A	WD 6/98
67. rolodex	Rolodex rotary card files	Newell Office Products	N, A	Donlan
68. saran wrap	Saran Wrap plastic film	Dow	N, V, A	
69. scotch tape	Scotch transparent tape	3M	N, V, A	Triplett
70. scotch guard, scotch gard	Scotchgard fabric protector	3M	N, V, A	
71. sharpie	Sparpie permanent marker	Sanford	N, A	
72. sheetrock, sheet rock	Sheetrock plaster wall board	USG	N, A	Lederer
73. slim jim	Slim Jim car opening tool for use by locksmiths	Reginald C. Potts	N, A	Lederer
74. slinky	Slinky spring toys	James	N, A	
75. spackle	Spackle surfacing compound	The Muralo Corp.	N, V, A	WD 3/98

76. spam	Spam luncheon meat	Hormel	N, A	WD 6/98
77. stairmaster	StairMaster exercise equipment	StairMaster Sports/Medical Products Inc.	N, A	WD 3/98
78. styrofoam	Styrofoam plastic foam	Dow	N, A	Donlan
79. sweet tarts	Sweetarts candy	Nestle	N, A	
80. tabasco sauce	Tabasco pepper sauce	McIlhenny Co.	N, A	
81. tampax	Tampax tampons	Tambrands Inc.	N, A	
82. tater tots	Tater Tots frozen shredded potatoes	Ore-Ida Foods	N, A	
83. technicolor	Technicolor motion picture films	Technicolor Inc.	N, A	
84. teflon	Teflon non-stick coating	Du Pont	N, A	Adams
85. teleprompter	Teleprompter	TelePromTer	N, A	Adams
86. thermos	Thermos vacuum flask container	King-Sealy Thermos Co.	N, A	
87. TV dinners	TV Dinner frozen dinners	Campbell Soup	N, A	Lederer
88. tylenol	Tylenol acetamino-phen	McNeill Consumer Products Co.	N, A	
89. ugli fruit	Ugli fruit	Cable Hall Citrus Co.	N, A	WD 9/97
90. valium	Valium diazepam	Roche	N, A	Adams
91. vaseline	Vaseline petrolium jelly	Cheesebor-ough-Ponds	N, A	Triplett

92. velcro	Velcro hook and loop fasteners	Velcro Ind.	N, V, A	WD 6/98
93. walkman	Walkman portable stereos	Sony Corp.	N, A	Donlan
94. weed eater, weedeater	WeedEater lawn trimmers	White Consolidated Industries	N, A	WD 11/97
95. white-out	Wite-Out correction fluid	Bic Corp.	N, V, A	WD 6/94
96. wiffle ball	Wiffle plastic balls	The Wiffle Ball Inc.	N, A	Lederer
97. windbreaker	Windbreaker jackets	The Windbreaker Co.	N, A	
98. exacto knife	X-Acto knives	X-Acto	N, A	
99. xerox	Xerox photocopiers	Xerox Corp.	N, V, A	
100. ziploc bag	Ziploc resealable bags	Dow	N, V, A	WD 9/93

APPENDIX B. TOKENS TO ESTABLISH GENERICIZATION IN CORPUS

1. Ace bandages   (Net)

1998   The silicone gel is cut slightly larger than the wound and covered with a Band-Aid, ace bandage, cloth wrap or tape. (www.capederm.com/info_silicone_gel.htm)

NA   The injury should be treated with cold packs and wrapped with an ace bandage. (www.global-fitness.com/article_pain.html)

2. Allen wrench   (Net)

1997   Each come with two eye hooks, two hex nut screws (to lock the two sides together) and an allen wrench. (www.sfdungeon.com/frdo0016.html)

1998   This is a variation on Park's Y-allen wrench, with the very excellent Bondhus balldriver system. (www.lickbike.com/i2613200)

Notes: Listed in OED.

3. AstroTurf   (OED) (Astrodome+turf)

1975   Campsites ... carpeted with astroturf.

1986   He couldn't wait to test the Bourbon Street Theory on the Superdome astroturf.

Notes: Alt. spellings astroturf, astro-turf. Listed as PA, A. Also examples given in N, V possible.

4. Baggies   (Net)

1999   Pack a collar and leash, treats and toys, extra water, and a cleanup kit of paper towels, plastic baggies, carpet cleaner. (www.seattletimes.com/news/lifestyles/html98/tips_081098.html)

1998   It took Rosa and the artist two full days to "paint" the walls using plastic baggies as their paint brushes. (www.rcinteriors.com/bagging.html)

5. **Bake-Off**   (Net)

    1998   Approximately 100 people participated in a Chili Bake-Off to
            honor Kyle Marchase on Saturday, Feb. 7, at the Brewery
            Restaurant in Honeoye Falls.
            (www.ourhometown.com/Sentinel/common/news/3398/comm5.
            html)

    1998   The annual Bake Off pits oven against oven as the tastiest treats in
            town are auctioned off to raise funds for BGF.
            (www.sydney.sidewalk.com.au/html/syd/018/18871.htm)

6. **Band-Aid**   (Net)

    1998   If you are having trouble keeping a band-aid on baby's boo-boo, try
            wrapping a second band-aid around her index finger.
            (ourworld.compuserve.com/homepages/celticbabies/index.htm)

    1998   Our band-aid stands for the emergency aid that is at the ready
            when your urgent need arises. (www.ipserv.com/BAID.HTML).

Notes: Listed in OED.

7. **Ben-Gay**   (Net)

    1998   It smells like a breath mint and makes your skin hot in the same
            way that ben-gay does.
            (www.bioch.ox.ac.uk/~jr/henna/discuss/messages/1074.html)

    1998   The heat is like when you put bengay on your legs, that kind of
            warmth without the bengay actually being on.
            (www.aboutwomen.com/emotional/messages/534.html)

8. **Bondo**   (Net)   (bond+-o)

    1996   V-8 and Powerglide transmission, this original California car has
            had no rust or bondo ever. (www.route66classics.com/chev4.htm)

    1998   Some bondo here and bondo there would help a little too.
            (www.house-of-poetry.com/comedypoem4.html)

9. **Brasso**   (Net)   (brass+-o)

    1997   I don't need to get them perfectly clean, they will not be re-plated, just a little polishing (brasso).
        (www.finishing.com/0800-0999/936.html)

    1998   to (sic) resurface the drum buy some brasso and get a cloth that is like cotton and go in a circular motion and polish the drum.
        (copynet.tinfox.com/forums/enduser/messages/879.html)

10. **Brillo** pad   (Net)   (brill+-o)

    1996   I was thinking of a brillo pad or something of that nature, but does anyone know if I should use something else?
        (www.contesting.com/_towertalk/9606/0102.html)

    1996   Did you use a brillo pad and some hydrochloric acid to clean it?
        (209.125.128.2/Feedback/GeneralArticles/
        Icantresistthisone.html.)

11. **Cat Chow**   (Net)

    1999   And which is better, cat or dog chow? (possumnetwork.com/faq-tech.htm)

    1998   Here's a list of things we are ALWAYS in need of: ..dry cat chow, paper towels, Kleenex..
        (www.worldwide-interads.com/ncspca/howhelp.htm)

12. **Chap Stick**   (Net)

    1998   When he got off the lift, he asked me to hold on because he needed to put on some chapstick. (www.weddingcreator.com/stories.htm)

    1998   Why do they call it chapstick?
        (www.basd.k12.pa.us/studpage/holly/facts/htm)

13. **Cheez Doodles**   (Net)

    1997   She read, "How Stella Got Her Groove Back", FROM COVER TO COVER while eating Little Debbie snack cakes and cheese doodles, and watching, "Days of Our Lives".
        (www.ims-1.com/writers/messages/1160.html)

194

1998 Alas 'tis also a Tuesday, so for most, the customary romping and
feasting shall be condensed into a 45 minute session with a bag of
cheese doodles.
(www.sfgate.com/offbeat/sevenDays/tuesday/tuesday.html)

14. **Cheez Whiz**   (Net)

1996 God only knows what it was about, but all of a sudden Dad started
yelling something about cheese whiz..
(www.stepstones.com/max617a.htm)

1996 I have a bachelor friend who is a cheese whiz addict.
(www.prz.tu-berlin.de/~nicolai/mealmaster/mailings/
MMrecipes/2300.html)

15. **Coke**   (OED) (cocaine)

1915 The propensity of a large proportion of those who regularly drink
Coca-Cola to call for their favorite drink as 'dope' or 'coke' or
'koke'.

1938 The girls drank 'coke' mostly.

16. **Cool Whip**   (Net)

1997 I have cream cheese,cool whip(sic), choc chips, coconut, and
cookies. (www.fatcafe.com/food/messages/520.html)

1998 Mix chunks, yogurt and cool whip.
(www.fatcatcafe.com/food/messages/522.html)

17. **Crayolas**   (Net)

1999 Maybe with blunt crayolas and poster paper we could show this
bass club's officers that a quarter pound penalty is precious little
deterrent to mishandling fish..
(www.texnews.com/1998/outdoors/jerry0531.html)

1999 Second, I really enjoy the paper table cloths complete with
crayolas for doodling love messages or drawing smiley faces.
(www.austin.citysearch.com/E/V/AUSTX/0001/52/61/)

18. **Crock-Pot**   (Net)

    1996   Put all ingrediants in except evaporated milk in crock pot.
             (www.thomasland.org/recip007.htm)

    1997   I need some new crock pot recipes ... relatively low fat ... for small
             crock pot! (chaski.com/wwwboard/food/messages/380.html)

19. **Dacron**   (OED) (Invented name)

    1957   His smiling teeth looked as repensively synthetic as his orlon shirt
             and dacron suit and nylon socks.

    1969   A dacron shirt and set of cotton-dacron underwear, good for quick
            and easy washing for the traveller.

20. **Day-Glo**   (OED) (day+glow)

    1959   The day-glo socks of the innumerable little girls.

    1960   There was..an undisclosed number of cloth 'dayglo' markers in
            geometric shapes.

Notes: 2nd meaning listed in OED, alt.spellings (day-glo, dayglo, dayglow, etc.)

21. **Dictaphone**   (OED) (dictate+phone)

    1907   The 'dictaphone' an adaptation of the phonograph.

    1920   A familiar object in many business and editorial offices is the
            dictaphone, an instrument which records on wax cylinders letters
            or articles spoken into it.

22. **Dixie Cups**   (Net)

    1998   ... loves koolaid when his mom makes it right and likes to drink it
             from a dixie cup.
             (www.snowcrest.net/landonh/messages/2854.html)

    1998   If you have some soap left over, pour into a dixie cup.
             (www.soapcrafters.com/recipec.htm)

23. **Dramamine**   (OED) (d(iphenhyd)ramine)+redup.)

    1958   Edgar, beginning to feel liverish and sleepy from the dramamine table he had punctiliously taken an hour before sailing.

               (Net)
    1996   She takes dramamine every day and thinks it may help a little. (dem0nmac.mgh.harvard.edu/neurowebforum/MultipleSclero.../Dr amamine.htm)

24. **Drano**   (Net)

    NA   All you need is some draino, water, and tin foil. (www.suresite.com/oh/z/zerocool/

    1997   Gene Laughter tried everything from bleach to draino to get the hardener out without success. (www.zilker.net/~gwalker/altphoto/alt97a/2358.html)

25. **Dumpster**   (Net)   (dump+-ster)

    1997   I looked behind my local grocery store and couldn't find a dumpster. What gives? (www.geocities.com/RainForest/1137/dumpdiv.htm)

    1998   (Dumpster diving) The practice of sifting refuse from an office or technical installation to extract confidential data, especially security-compromising information ('dumpster' is an Americanism for what is elsewhere called a 'skip'). (www.wins.uva.nl/~mes/jargon/d/dumpsterdiving.html)

26. **Federal Express** (Net)

    1997   Finally, after a lot of haggling and "are you sure"s (sic), they came up with a procedure whereby we federal expressed a couple of blank credit card slips..to the train staion in Toronto, and they'd send us some CanRail passes, so we could Federal Express the CanRail passes back. (www.drbanks.com/Canada/preparations.html)

    1998   My mother federal expressed a large box of fall leaves from Chicago to the West Portal branch of the Comm Tech Lab. (commtechlab.msu.edu/humans/heeter/portalreports/ch11-24/ ch11-22.html)

27. **Fiberglas**   (OED) (fiber+glass)

    1941   A fabric made of 'fibre glass' for wing covering.

    1951   A quilt of fibre glass between the bedroom ceiling and the roof gives protection against cold.

Notes: fibreglass, fibre-glass, fiberglass, fibre-glass all listed in OED.

28. **Fig Newtons**   (Net)

    1998   By long tradition, each meeting begins with fifteen minutes of informal conversation in the department lounge (Science 2400) over chips, salsa, and fig newtons ... (www.math.grin.edu/journal-club.html)

    1999   In emergencies, I've broken open a package of fig newtons and handed her one as I race downthe (sic) aisles! (www.thebabynet.com/babytalkpages/messages/breastfeeding/417 8.html)

29. **Formica**   (OED) (for mica 'a resin')

    1957   Red upholstered chairs with chromium legs and tables in formica.

    1959   One tinselly formica-and-chrome establishment.

30. **Freon**   (OED)

    1945   Insulation is provided by freon gas.

    1950   The structures of most of the 'Freons' having from one to five carbon atoms.

31. **Frigidaire**   (OED) (Lat. frigidarium)

    1926   Vacuum cleaners, frigidaires, radios.

    1940   And had everything necessary to the Modern Man, A gramophone, a radio, a car, and a frigidaire.

32. **Frisbee**   (OED) (Frisbie Bakery)

   1969   The frisbee..is a plastic disc about the size of a frying pan that in
          the hands of the experts out boomerangs the boomerang.

   1971   Gunny-sacked racers hobble about and frisbee circles form.

Notes: Also listed as frisby.

33. **Gore-Tex**   (Net)   (W.L. Gore+Textiles)

   1996   I also have a goretex coat and helmet cover.
          (cycling.org/lists/mtb/mtb-archive-hyper/mtb.9602/0262/html)

   1996   With goretex cables you have to be a little more cautious.
          (www.cyclery.com/lists/mtb-trials/mtb-trials-archive-
          hyper/mtb-trials.9611/0298.html)

34. **Hi-Liter**   (Net)   (highlight+-er)

   1996   Yes, I made this entire fabulous painting using ONLY yellow,
          green, orange, blue and pink hi-liters.
          (www.csusm.edu/public/guests/priestss/hiliter.htm)

   NA   If you have printer access, print the page and use a hi-liter.
          (geocities.com/HotSprings/3055/puzzles2.html)

35. **Hovercraft**   (OED) (hover+craft)

   1965   Air cushion vehicles------or hovercraft, if you prefer the term.

   1967   Designed initially for military logistic-support duties, the BH 8 is a
          twin-engined, 80 ton, open-water hovercraft with bow and stern
          loading doors.

Notes: OED says lost protection and is common.

36. **Hula Hoop**   (Net)

   1997   When your group gets really good at this game place 2 or 3 hula
          hoops in the circle. (www.cais.net/cwelch/gsrc/game0630.htm)

   1997   A year later almost nobody seemed interested in hula hoops.
          (www.infoworld.com/cgi-bin/displayNew.pl?/lewis/980413rl.htm)

37. **Jacuzzi** (OED)

1973 You'll hear this kind of pool called a 'Jacuzzi', because the Jacuzzi firm pioneered in this application of the hydro-jet.

1976 Hawaii Kai: luxury 1 bdrm, oceanview, pool jacuzzis & saunas.

38. **Jeep** (OED)

1941 Beer wagons moved on the road with the brown jeeps of G.P. (General Purpose) soldiers and marines.

1942 The light armoured car which hauls the gun and carries the gun crew is called a jeep.

39. **Jell-O** (OED) (jelly+-o)

1936 Nervous pudding, Shivering Liz, or Shimmy for jello..describe neatly.

1961 All the side dishes of salad and jello were there.

40. **Jockey shorts** (OED)

1951 I remember in 1932 telling Truman to stick to the haberdashery business, that there was a fortune in shirts and jockey shorts.

1968 I took to wearing tight jockey shorts.

41. **Kitty Litter** (Net)

1998 The bottom line is that all cat food and kitty-litter boxes need to be inaccessible to your dog. (www.doggiedoor.com/catlitte.htm)

1998 His bath tub is a small kitty litter box. (www.robinsfyi.com/boa.htm)

42. **Kleenex** (OED) (clean+-ex)

1997 How do you make a kleenex dance? (www.datasync.com/~tree/jokes/messages/2.html)

1998 Would someone get me a kleenex? (www.theromancereader.com/sparks-notebook.html)

43. **Kool-Aid** (Net)

> 1999 My 10 year old daughter twin granddaughters want me to dye of strip of their hair using kool-aid.
> (www.thathomesite.com/forums/load/parents/msg0807050826211.html)

> 2000 My friend is a koolaide dyer.
> (www.thathomesite.com/forums/load/parents/msg0807050826211.html)

44. **Laundromat** (OED) (laundry+-mat)

> 1951 The Westinghouse Company has a 'Laundramat', and there are also 'Laundromats'--often called 'Laundermats' and 'Laundrymats--open for public patronage.

> 1955 The village mind was still churning up the past, tossing the old dirty linen back and forth impersonally, like one of the washing machines in the new laundromat.

45. **Levi's** (OED) (Levi Strauss)

> 1944 Blue jeans ('levis') or corduroys, rolled at the bottom, are worn by almost all boys.

> 1957 Dean was wearing washed-out tight levis and a T-shirt.

Notes: Also lists Levis, Levi, Levies.

46. **Lifesavers** (Net)

> 1998 You are a color or flavor in a package of lifesavers. What color or flavor would you be and why? (ohomxiv.org/ohkd95c8.htm)

> 1999 Then one day, the teacher brought in a great variety of lifesavers, more flavors than you could ever imagine.
> (www.isip.com/users/kealoha/lifesavers.htm)

47. Lycra   (OED)

1963   Proofed..lycra jersey ski pants.

1968   This..pantie-corselette..of softest lycra power net.

48. Mace   (OED)

1968   Scores of innocent bystanders..were clubbed, maced, arrested.

1969   The stuff was..some kind of chemical Mace or nerve gas.

Notes: Verb usage also listed.

49. Magic Marker   (OED)

1973   With chalk, magic markers, but most often with..aerosol spray paint, the pitch was marked out with slogans.

1988   She highlighted in yellow magic marker the books and articles recommended by Jeanne.

50. Milk-Bone   (Net)

1995   If I had a milk bone I'd chew it in the morning. (www.cybermind.org.hk/archive/cybermind.0695/0620.html)

NA   Contradicting what I just said, a nutrional long lasting milk bone treat given when you leave may divert her attention and help her calm herself. (lowellg.simplenet.com/faq25.htm)

51. Muzak   (OED) (Kodak + music)

1965   We shall have muzak wherever we go.

1968   If muzak be the food of love, no wonder it is commonly to be found..among the frozen mint-flavored peas and crinkle-cut chips.

Notes: Musak, muzakal (Adj.) or muzakman, V Muzaked also listed.

202

52. **Novocain** (OED) (Lat. nov(us)+(c)ocain)

   1910 For regional anaestesia novocain has given good results.

   1926 Mrs. Mary Agnes Brown..died..following injections of cocaine hydrochlorate, which had been mistakenly administered instead of novocain solution.

53. **NutraSweet** (Net) (nutra-+sweet)

   1996 When I cut out caffeine and cola and nutrisweet I seem to get a little better and a lot calmer. (dem0nmac.mgh.harvard.edu/neurowebforum/Alzh.../ Notsoyoungwmemoryproblems.htm)

   1997 I've been wondering if drinking so much diet soda (some caffinated, some not) is smart, given the nutrisweet arguments.. (zonehome.com/zt10/_disc/0000005d.htm)

54. **Pine Sol** (Net) (pine+solvent)

   NA He smells like pinesol, and is the pimp of the troupe. (www.angelfire.com/me feeble/index.html)

   1998 It used ammonia, pinesol and 20 mule team borax. (www.hcampers.com/hcbbs/891830419043.html)

55. **Ping-Pong** (OED)

   1902 To have your squash-court this summer, if you have any pretensions to style, is as necessary as to have your ping-pong table or your automobile.

   1907 A set of 'ping-pong' materials.

Notes: 1949 Official Gaz. (U.S. Patent Office) 4 Oct. 40/2 Parker Brothers, Inc., Salem, Mass. .. Ping-pong ... For game played with rackets and balls. Claims use since Aug. 1, 1900.

56. **Plexiglas** (OED) (plexi-+-glass)

   1943 The sergeant had carved the handles of his gun from the plexiglass from the nose of a bomber.

1951   Roof, tar and gravel with plexiglass skylights.

57. **Polaroid**   (OED)

1976   Two polaroid colour photographs of a dark-haired man.

(Net)

1999   If you were wondering what kinds of injustice digital scans of polaroids could do to a friendly face, look at our collection of department pictures below. (landau1.phys.virginia.edu/info/people/pboard/)

58. **Pop-Tarts**   (Net)

1997   Snackwells now has a lower-fat version of pop tarts that my wife says are more tasty. (www.cyclery.com/lists/ultra/ultra-archive-hyper/ultra.9701/0118.html)

1998   He lives on nothing but pop-tarts and beer, and his body shows it. (thewebweaver.com/)

59. **Porta Potti**   (Net) (portable+potty)

1997   Registration is $10 and lets you participate in two races (it also gives you porta-potty privleges). (newsobserver.com/nao/go/entrec/whatsup/062097/check620.html)

1997   It will hold a concert grand..with room for my porta-potti too. (www.tns.lcs.mit.edu/harp/archives/1997.01/0520.html)

60. **Post-it notes**   (Net)

1996   Sticky Notes-- This is the computerized version of those little yellow sticky post-it notes. (cws.avalon.nf.ca/16phone-sticky.html)

1998   Put up a post-it note for All to see. E-mail us with your message and we'll put it up on this page. (www.discworks.com/post.html)

61. **Pyrex**   (OED) (invented word)

1927   Housewives no longer use iron pots and pans. Their kitchenettes are bright with aluminum and pyrex ware.

1932   Tea was served, Poured by the secretary from a pyrex teapot.

62. Q-Tips   (Net)

1998   ..then have the children dip the q-tip into the paint.
       (www.artswire.org/kenroar/lessons/early/early17.html)

1998   Her favorite game involves q-tips. (www.etropolis.com/msz)

63. ReaLemon   (Net)   (real+lemon)

1998   In bowl combine: 2 eggs, 1/2 cup sugar, 1/3 cups real lemon.
       (www.bbonline.com/~bbonline/mi/atchison/recipe1.html)

NA   Add water, real lemon juice, & egg yolk; mix well.
       (www.deter.com/flora/mxp/pie/229.html)

64. Realtor   (OED) (realty+-or)

1922   We ought to insist that folks call us 'realtors' and not 'real-estate
       men'. Sounds more like a reg'lar profession.

1925   These realtors, as they call themselves, I presume are influential.

65. Rice Krispies   (OED)

1956   The fourteen-year old at the breakfast table..can devour the Black
       Mass with her rice crispies.

1963   The mouse..eats a Rice Crispy like a sandwich.

Notes: Also listed as rice crispies, Rice Crispy.

66. Rollerblade   (OED) (roller+blade)

1989   Examples ranged from windsurfing and rollerblade skating to
       jogging and wallyball.

1991   One cruises on a bike, one coasts on roller blades, three ride
       skateboards.

Notes: Verb also listed.

67. **Rolodex**   (Net)   (rolling+index?)

    1995   The advantage of using the rolodex over direct "dialing" is that a tool intersection is calculated.
           (quasi.stanford.edu/collab/collab_help.html)

    1998   TBN's Rolodex (www.tbn.org/ministry/ministry.htm)

68. **Saran Wrap**   (Net)

    1998   Roll up as a "jelly roll" and wrap in wax paper, saran wrap, or foil.
           (www.blessing2.com/auntappe.html)

    1998   Douglas McIver applies marinade to beef tenderloin, then wraps tightly in saran wrap to marinate in the refrigerator.
           (www.cookshack.com/ne06010.html)

Notes: Verb usage also listed.

69. **Scotch tape**   (OED)

    1947   Electrical grade scotch tape is widely used for anchoring leads.

    1955   There was a wire, scotch-taped to the upper side of the bag.

Notes: Verb usage also listed.

70. **Scotchgard**   (Net)   (scotch+guard)

    1996   If you get a new rig, coat it with two cans of spray scotch-gard.
           (www.afn.org/skydive/usenet/1996/aug/0424.html)

    1996   I've been reading your advice regarding first rigs, and wanna ask you about the spray scotch-gard you mention. What is this stuff, and where you can (sic) get it?. Does it have a Brand Name?. (sic)
           (www.afn.org/skydive/usenet/1996/aug/0424.html)

71. **Sharpie**   (Net)   (sharp+-ie)

    1998   Official Remo drum head signed in-person in gold sharpie by reggae star Ziggy Marley.
           (www.celebritykeepsakes.com/musicmemorabilia.htm)

1998   Old style Orange Broncos jersey signed in blue sharpie $369.
(www.mos-sports.com/fball/Elway.html)

72. Sheetrock   (Net)   (sheet+rock)

1996   My question is should a plastic vapor barrier be placed on the walls
before the sheetrock goes on?
(www.aecinfo.com/forum/wb07/messages/93.html)

1998   I.T.R. Acoustic Drywall Inc. Construction firm specializes in the
installation of interior and exterior steel-stud framing, sheet rock,
all types of ceilings, insulation, sound proofing.
(www.itr-can-usa.com/index1.htm)

73. Slim Jim   (Net)

1997   We understand that there was a fatal accident involving the use of a
slim jim recently on the mainland.
(leahi.kcc.hawaii.edu/bulletin/announce/2223.html)

1998   Many older automobiles can still be opened with a Slim Jim type
of opener..
(www.montana.com/people/home1/xwrathx/www/cookbook/
004.TXT)

74. Slinky   (OED) (slink+-y)

1975   The tangled slinky toy lives of these three turned-on folk heroes.

         (Net)

1995   She was buying clothes, and I was putting slinkies on the
escalators.   (lalaland.cl.msu.edu/~vanhoose/humor/0297.html)

75. Spackle   (OED) (Ger. spachtel 'putty knife')

1951   You must be sure there is paint on the surface upon which you are
going to put the spackle.

1971   After he did that he mixed the spackle with water and spread it as
evenly as he could over the crack.

Notes: Also verb listed with additional sense.

76. **Spam**   (OED) (spiced+ham)

    1942   There, arrayed in all their glory, were slices of ham, spam, bologna and potato salad.

            (Net)

    1998   If you want rolled sushi style spam, then the cooked spam is sliced into long strips.
            (www.neosoft.com/recipes/asian/spam-musubi.html)

77. **StairMaster**   (Net)   (stair+master)

    1996   What are the five most important things to think about when using the stairmaster?
            (lifematters.com/lm/messagesft3/451.html)

    1999   Monday through Friday -- 30 minutes on the treadmill (..), 10 minutes on the stairmaster.
            (members.xoom.com/Debashis_Nag/exercise.htm)

78. **Styrofoam**   (OED) (polystyrene+-o-+foam)

    1962   How to make..lambs from glass fibre, angels from styrofoam.

    1969   Insulated container, Rectangular, styrofoam insulation between aluminum panels.

79. **Sweetarts**   (Net)   (sweet+tarts)

    1997   Eventually the kid settled for this candy which was like a pack of sweet tarts with a lolly-pop stick going through the center of all of them. (www.syr.edu/~bjmctear/d44.html)

    1998   She's cute and gives me smarties and sweet tarts.
            (www.edgeculture.net/karkajou/pursuits.html)

80. **Tabasco sauce**   (OED) (Mexican river and state)

    1876   The popular drinks..were all made from the same bad rum, worse tobasco, and first-class cayenne.

1902   Mix with due assiduity, and finally add from drops of tabasco.

Notes: Not trademarked until 1902.

81. **Tampax**   (Net)   (tampon+packs)

1998   What are the pros and cons of using either tampons or tampax? (www.korealink.com/public/sex/messages/356.htm)

1999   The difference is much the same as that between a tampax and a super-tampax. (www.cs.uq.oz.au/personal/bof/Supermodel/intro.html)

82. **Tater Tots**   (Net)

1998   Tuesday - Fish sandwich or chicken patty on a bun, tater tots, carrot and celery sticks, fresh fruit in season. (www.naplesnews.com/today/neopolitan/d227238a.htm)

1998   Cover top with tater tots. (www.pastrywiz.com/archive/buddies.htm)

Notes: Trademarked in 1949.

83. **Technicolor**   (OED) (technical+color)

1940   The theme..would come in some such guise as the auto horns from the Technicolor boulevards below.

1946   She looked very beautiful, and in glorious technicolour.

84. **Teflon**   (Net)   (polytetrafluoroethylene)

1996   Then they apply a thin layer of adhesive which is mixed with a small amount of teflon. (www.shu.ac.uk/schools/sci/sol/cgi/answers/setahd02.htm)

1998   Our most popular service is the acrylic teflon sealant, "no wax" warranty program.   (www.colormatchintl.com/sealant.html)

85. **Teleprompter**   (OED)

1958   Last night he seemed to be using a teleprompter, so rapidly did the words rattle out.

1961   That's what the boys in the backroom had written, and it was staring at him..from the teleprompter.

Notes: Formerly a brand name in U.S. says OED.

86. **Thermos**   (OED) (gr. thermos 'hot')

1922   Say, could I borrow your thermos--just dropped in to see if I could borrow your thermos bottle.

1923   I'd got my thermos filled the day before.

Note: OED reports as still a trademark (1984). Hence loosely applied to any vacuum flask.

87. **TV Dinners**   (Net)

1998   MAKE HEALTHY TV DINNERS!!
(www.interking.com/b/h/tv_dinners.html)

1999   The sole purpose of this page is the expression of a critical review of TV dinners. (includes list of TV dinners by more than a dozen different companies). (www.yarayara.com/tv/tvtable.html)

88. **Tylenol**   (Net)

1996   I've tried salt, pickles, tylenol, aspirin, salt water, lysine (a mineral) and vitamin C.
(www.netguard.net/~drweed/wwwboard/archives/messages/675.htm)

1997   Gabapentin added to her depakote and tylenol has helped her in this, and has also allowed us to decrease her tylenol to almost none.
(www.neuro.wustl.edu/wwwboard/newmessages/3651.html)

89. **Ugli fruit**   (OED) (ugly fruit)

1958   Passion fruit, mangoes, uglifruit, and pomegranates.

1975   Prince Charles loves an ugli, so said the Queen when she opened London's new Covent Garden market recently.

210

90. **Valium**   (OED) (arbitrary name)

 1976   I have been swallowing fistfuls of valium to try to calm myself.

 (Net)

 NA   My physician tells me not to worry because the amount of valium
        is minimal. (preganancytoday.com/experts/lc/bfvalium.htm)

91. **Vaseline**   (OED) (Ger. wasser+ Gr. elaion 'oil')

 1876   Applied vaseline to his head whenever the cap was off.

 1884   Palm oil and vaseline was sold for lubricating machinery.

92. **Velcro**   (OED) (Fr. velours+crochet)

 1961   We have been experimenting for some time with the new Bri-
        nylon fastener, 'velcro', using it particularly for patients who have
        difficulty in doing up buttons, trousers and belts.

 1971   They had dressed him in a blue sleepcoat, which..was secured up
        the front by a strip of velcro.

93. **Walkman**   (OED)

 1998   I'm falling in love, with my walkman and me.
        (www.compusmart.ab.ca/veruca/davidbowielyrics.html)

 1998   I missed the start of this thread, but the cheapest possible guitar
        amp (IMHO) is to fee the output of your guitar into the input of a
        Walkman-type cassette player.
        (www.harmony-central.com/Guitar/walkman-amp.txt)

94. **Weed Eater**   (Net)

 1999   I have a Homelite weedeater and I can (sic) seem to adjust the
        Carburator to get any power at all.
        (www.homeownernet.com/chat/messages/121.html)

 1998   I could really use some advice on buying the best of heavy duty
        weedeaters. (207.159.53.230/toolt/messages/644.html)

95. **Wite-Out**　　　(Net)　(white+out)

NA　　I got white-out here; three bucks a pop; good quality stuff; who needs white-out? (hubcap.clemson.edu/~tmuntz/round6.htm)

NA　　How can you tell if a blonde's been using the computer? There's white-out on the screen. (users.intercomm.com/chadt/humor/blonde04.html)

96. **Wiffle ball**　　　(OED)

1970　[David Eisenhower] passing the afternoon playing wiffle ball on the south lawn of his father-in-law's White House.

1985　Some people use the term Wiffle Ball for any plastic ball.

97. **Windbreaker**　　　(Net)　(wind+breaker)

NA　　Always bring a dry change of clothes, woolsweater, windbreaker, eyeglass strap and sneakers. (www.eideti.com/sports/pwa/details.html)

1998　60's Nylon racing stripe windbreaker $38. (www.jimsvintage.com/hotitems.htm)

98. **X-Acto**　　　(Net)

1998　Using a sharp exacto knife or razor saw, cut the door at the left edge where it joins the tapered wall. (www.polarlights.com/list_jupiterfix.html)

1998　Is there any way to use the exacto knife with out scratching the glass. www.artglasswrold.com/wwwboard/messages/1956.html)

99. **Xerox**　　　(OED) (xerography+-x)

1966　In most American offices executives instruct subordinates to 'make me a Xerox of this report' rather than 'make me a copy of it'.

1972　The Rank Organization in Brighton installed a xerox copying machine in the office and we also had an electric duplicating machine.

100. **Ziploc bags**   (Net)   (zip+lock)

    1997   I also place the dried peppers in ziploc bags for preservation. (www.sammcgees.com/chili/brd/messages/16.html)

    1998   This Dear is brand new and stored in a ziploc bag. (www.cityauction.com/items/160547

REFERENCES

Adams, Thomas. 1987. Trademarks. English Today 9, 34.

Aitchison, Jean. 1981. Language change: Progress or decay? London: Fontana.

Alford, Richard. 1987. Naming and identity: A cross-cultural study of personal naming practices. New Haven, CT: HRAF Press.

Aronoff, Mark. 1998. Review of American automobile names, by Ingrid Piller. Lg. 74(3), 658.

Ashley, Leonard. 1989. What's in a name? Baltimore: Genealogical Publishing Company Inc.

Bainton, George. 1890. The art of authorship. Literary reminiscences, methods of work, and advice to young beginners. London: James Clarke & Co.

Baron, Dennis. 1989. Word law. Verbatim 16(1). 1-4.

Basso, Keith. 1990. Western Apache language and culture. Tucson: The University of Arizona Press.

Bender, Byron. 1970. An Oceanic place-name study. Pacific Linguistic Studies in Honour of Arthur Capell, ed. by Stephen A. Wurm and Donald E. Laycock, 165-88. Sydney: A.H. & A.W. Reed.

Berlin, Brent, and Paul Kay. 1969. Basic color terms: Their universality and evolution. Berkeley: University of California Press.

Bloomfield, Leonard. 1933. Language. London: George Allen & Unwin.

Blust, Robert. 1988. Austronesian root theory. Philadelphia: John Benjamins Publishing Company.

Bolinger, Dwight. 1980. Language: The loaded weapon. London: Longman.

Borchard, William. 1995. Trademark basics: A guide for business. New York: International Trademark Association.

Brown, Roger. 1973. A first language : the early stages.Cambridge, MA: Harvard University Press.

Brown, Cecil. 1984. Language and living things: Uniformities in folk classification and naming. New Brunswick, NJ: Rutgers University Press.

Brown, Cecil, and Stanley Witkowski. 1981. Figurative language in a universalist perspective. American Ethnologist 8(3). 596-615.

Buranen, Lise and Alice Roy. 1999. Perspectives on plagiarism and intellectual property in the post-modern world. Albany, NY: SUNY Press.

Cannon, Garland. 1995. Innovative Japanese Borrowings in English. Dictionaries: Journal of the Dictionary Society of America 16:90-101.

Carroll, John. 1985. What's in a name? An essay in the psychology of reference. New York: W.H. Freeman and Company.

Carroll, Lewis. 1872. Through the looking-glass. London: MacMillan and Company.

Catfish by any other name. 2002 (February). Time (Asian Edition), 14-15.

Chan, Allen and Yue Huang. 1997. Brand naming in China: a linguistic approach. Marketing Intelligence & Planning 15(5). 227-34.

Charmasson, Henri. 1988. The name is the game. Homewood, IL: Dow Jones-Irwin.

Clankie, Shawn. 1999. Generic brand name use in creative writing: Trademark misuse and genericide or language right? Perspectives on plagiarism and intellectual property in the post-modern world, ed. by Alice Roy and Lise Buranen. Albany: SUNY Press.

Clankie, Shawn. 2001. Domain names, cybersquatters, and the law: Who's to blame? Journal of Information Ethics, 10(1), 27-34.

Cohen, Bob. 1998. There's more to a name. Linguistics at work: A reader of applications, ed. by Dallin D. Oaks. Ft. Worth: Harcourt Brace.

Conklin, Harold. 1955. Hanunoo Color Categories. Southwestern Journal of Anthropology 11: 339-44.

-------. 1964. Reprint of Hanunoo Color Categories. Language in Culture and Society ed. by Dell Hymes. New York: Harper & Row Publishers. 189-92.

-------. 1980. Folk Classification. Department of Anthropology, Yale University.

Crystal, David. 1994. An encyclopedia of linguistics. Cambridge: CUP.

Einstein, Albert 1936, Physics and Reality. Journal of the Franklin Institute, 221.

Federal Trademark Dilution Act of 1995. 1995. 15 USC 1051. U.S. statutes at large. Vol. 109 Pt. 1, 109 Stat. 985-87.

Finn, Michael. 1993 (September). Wite and proper usage. Writer's Digest. 64-7.

-------. 1995 (June). Beware of how you color it. Writer's Digest. 57-60.

Fishman, Joshua. 1991. Reversing language shift. Philadelphia: Multilingual Matters Ltd.

Fitch, G. W. 1987. Naming and believing. Dordecht: D. Reidel Publishing Company.

Frake, Charles. 1961. The diagnosis of disease among the Subanun of Mindinao. American Anthropologist 63:113-32.

216

Frake, Charles. 1962. The ethnographic study of cognitive systems. Anthropology and Human Behavior. Washington, D.C.: Anthropological Society of Washington.

-------. 1969. Reprint of The ethnographic study of cognitive systems. Cognitive Anthropology ed. by Stephen A. Tyler. New York: Holt, Rinehart and Winston, Inc. 28-41.

Frege, Gottlob. 1970. Translations from the philosophical writings of Gottlob Frege. Oxford: Basil Blackwell.

Friedman, Monroe. 1985. The changing language of a consumer society: Brand name usage in popular American novels in the postwar era. Journal of Consumer Research 11.927-38.

-------. 1986a. Brand-name use in news columns of American newspapers since 1964. Journalism Quarterly 63.161-66.

-------. 1986b. Commercial influences in popular literature: An empirical study of brand name usage in American and British hit plays in the postwar era. Empirical Studies of the Arts 4(1).63-77.

-------. 1991. A "brand" new language. New York: Greenwood Press.

Goddard, Cliff, and Anna Wierzbicka. 1994. Introducing lexical primitives. Semantic and lexical universals: Theory and empirical findings. Philadelphia: John Benjamins.

Grace, George. 1993. What are languages? Ethnolinguistics Notes, Series 3, Number 45. http://www2.hawaii.edu/usr-cgi/ssis/~grace/elniv6.html.

-------. 1997. The individual's knowledge of language and the traditional notion of languages. Ethnolinguistics Notes, Series 4, Number 7. http://www2.hawaii.edu/usr-cgi/ssis/~grace/elniv7.html.

-------. 1997b. How does "the language" change? Ethnolinguistics Notes, Series 4, Number 8. http://www2.hawaii.edu/usr-cgi/ssis/~grace/elniv8.html.

Grimm, Jakob Ludwig Karl. 1967. Rumpelstiltskin. New York: Harcourt, Brace & World.

Havelock, Eric. 1986. The muse learns to write. New Haven, CT: Yale University Press.

Headland, Thomas, Kenneth Pike, and Marvin Harris. 1990. Emics and Etics: The insider/outsider debate. Frontiers in Anthropology 7, Beverly Hills, CA: Sage Publications.

Hinton, Leanne, Johanna Nichols, and Ohala, John J. 1994. Sound symbolism. Cambridge: Cambridge University Press.

Hockett, Charles F. 1947. Problems of morphemic analysis. Lg. 23.321-43.

-------. 1958. A course in modern linguistics. New York: MacMillan Company.

Hoijer, Harry. 1954. Language and culture. The American Anthropological Association. Vol. 56, No. 6, Part 2, Memoir No. 79.

Householder, Fred. 1946. On the problem of sound and meaning, an English phonestheme. Word 2:83ff.

Hughes, Geoffrey. 1988. Words in time: A social history of the English vocabulary. Oxford: Basil Blackwell.

Hughes, Pennethorne. 1961. How you got your name: The origin and meaning of surnames. London: Phoenix House.

Jakobson, Roman and Linda Waugh. 1979. The sound shape of language. Bloomington, IN: Indiana University Press.

Jennings, Lane. 1981. Brave new worlds: Alternative futures for the English language. The Futurist, 15(3), 7-15.

Jespersen, Otto. 1965. The philosophy of grammar. New York: Norton Press.

Kaplan, Justin, and Anne Bernays. 1997. The language of names. New York: Simon & Schuster.

Kotler, Phillip, and Gary Armstrong. 1997. Marketing: An introduction (4th ed.). Englewood Cliffs, NJ: Prentice-Hall.

Kuwayama, Yasaburo. 1973. Trademarks & symbols volume 1: Alphabetical designs. New York: Van Nostrand Reinhold Company.

Landau, Sidney. 1994. Dictionaries: The art and craft of lexicography (2nd ed.). New York: Charles Scribner's Sons.

Lederer, Richard. 1985. Brand new eponyms. Verbatim 12(1). 1-2.

Lentine, Genine, and Roger Shuy. 1990. MC-: Meaning in the marketplace. American Speech 65(4).349-66.

Madrid Protocol Implementation Act. 1997. Report. Washington, D.C. United States Government Printing Office.

Madrid Protocol Implementation Act; And Trademark Law Treaty Implementation Act. 1997. Serial No. 7. Washington, D.C. United States Government Printing Office.

Mandelbaum, David. 1949. Selected writings of Edward Sapir. Berkeley, CA: University of California Press.

Martin, Laura. 1986. Eskimo words for snow: A case study in the genesis and decay of an anthropological example. American Anthropologist 88, 2 (June), 418-23.

Matthews, Peter. 1991. Morphology (2nd ed.). Cambridge: CUP.

McMahon, April. 1994. Understanding language change. Cambridge: CUP.

McCarthy, Edmund. 1987. Basic marketing: A managerial approach (9th ed.). Homewood,IL: Irwin.

Meillet, Antoine. 1912. Linguistique historique et linguistique generale. Paris: Champion.

Nietzche, Friederich Willhem. [1887] tr. 1967. On the genealogy of morals. New York: Vintage Books.

Nuessel, Frank. 1992. The study of names: A guide to the principles and topics. Westport, CT: Greenwood Press.

Oaks, Dallin D. 1997. Linguistics at work: A reader of applications. Ft. Worth: Harcourt Brace.

Oathout, John. 1981. Trademarks: A guide to the selection, administration and protection of trademarks in modern business practice. New York: Charles Scribner's Sons.

Ong, Walter. 1982. Orality and literacy: The technologizing of the word. New York: Methuen.

Oxford English Dictionary. 1989. Oxford: Oxford University Press.

Patton, Warren. 1980. An author's guide to the copyright law. Lexington, MA: Lexington Books.

Pike, Kenneth. 1954. Language in relation to a unified theory of the structure of human behavior. Glendale, CA: Summer Institute of Linguistics.

Piller, Ingrid. 1996. American automobile names. Essen: Die Blaue Eule.

Pulgram, Ernst. 1954. Theory of names. Berkely: American Name Society.

Pullum, Geoffrey. 1991. The great Eskimo vocabulary hoax and other irreverent essays on the study of language. Chicago: University of Chicago Press.

Room, Adrian. 1982. Dictionary of trade name origins. London: Routledge & Kegan Paul.

Room, Adrian. 1987. History of branding. Branding: A key marketing tool, ed. by John M. Murphy. London: The MacMillen Press Ltd., 13-21.

Russell, Bertrand. 1956. Logic and knowledge: Essays 1901-1950. London: George Allen and Unwin.

Sanders, Deborah. 1996 (June 1). Master of your domain. Success. 54.

Sapir, Edward. 1931. Conceptual categories in primitive languages. Science 74: 578.

Salzmann, Zedenek. 1993. Language, culture, & society: An introduction to linguistic anthropology. Boulder, CO: Westview Press.

Saussure, Ferdinand de. 1911. Lecture on General Linguistics.

Saussure, Ferdinand de. 1983. Course in general linguistics (English translation by R. Harris). London: Duckworth.

Schecter, Frank. 1925. The historical foundations of the law relating to trade-marks. New York: Columbia University Press.

Shibatani, Masayoshi. 1991. The languages of Japan. Cambridge: Cambridge University Press.

Smith-Bannister, Scott. 1997. Names and naming patterns in England 1538-1700. Oxford: Clarendon Press.

Stanlaw, James. 1992. "For beautiful human life" The use of English in Japan. Re-made in Japan: Everyday life and consumer taste in a changing society, ed. by Joe Tobin. New Haven: Yale University Press.

Stewart, Susan. 1991. Crimes of writing. New York: Oxford University Press.

Takashi, Kyoko. 1992. Language and desired identity in contemporary Japan. Journal of Asian Pacific Communication 3(1).133-44.

Tankard, James W. Jr. 1975. The effects of advertising on language: Making the sacred profane. Journal of Popular Culture 9(1), 325-30.

Terez, Angela. 1994 (November). Tricks of the trade(marks). Writer's Digest, 24-8.

Tobin, Joe. 1992. Re-made in Japan: Everyday life and consumer taste in a changing society. New Haven: Yale UP.

Trademark Checklist. 1994. New York: International Trademark Association.

Trademark Law Revision Act of 1988. 1988. United States statutes at large. 15USC 1051, Washington, D.C.: United States Government Printing Office. 102 Stat. 3935-48.

Trademarks: The official media guide. 1993. New York: International Trademark Association.

Tsur, Reuven. 1987. How do the sound patterns know they are expressive? Tel Aviv: Israel Science Publishers.

Ullmann, Stephen. 1962. Semantics: An introduction to the science of meaning. Oxford: Blackwell.

Vanden Bergh, Bruce, et al. 1984. Sound advice on brand names. Journalism Quarterly 64 (4).835-40.

Webster, Charles. no date. Survey evidence in trade mark and passing-off cases A valuable contribution or an exercise in futility? http://www.spoor.co.za/lib/survey.html.

Weinreich, Uriel, William Labov, and Marvin Herzog. 1968. Empirical foundations for a theory of language change. Directions for historical linguistics: A symposium, ed. by Winfred P. Lehmann and Yakov Malkiel. Austin, Texas: University of Texas Press.

Whorf, Benjamin Lee. 1952. Collected papers on metalinguistics. Washington, D.C.: Foreign Service Institute.

Yanabu, Akira. 1996. The Tenno system as the symbol of the culture of translation. Japan Review 7.147-57.

Zipf, Geo. 1935. The psycho-biology of language. 2nd ed. Boston: Houghton Mifflin Company.

Zorc, R. David, and Rachel San Miguel. 1991. Tagalog slang dictionary. Kensington, MD: Dunwoody Press.

STUDIES IN ONOMASTICS